"You will fall in love with *Barefoo̶ ̶ ̶ ̶ ̶ ̶ ̶ ̶ ̶ ̶ Ground.* You will fall in love with the author. You will fall in love with the children and friends you meet in its pages. But most importantly, you will fall in love with God, whether for the first time . . . or all over again."

—Bob Hostetler
Award-winning author and radio commentator
Author of *Beyond Belief to Convictions* (with Josh McDowell)

"This book is balm to the spirit of anyone hungering to know God intimately as their heavenly Daddy. Through literature, Scripture, story, and practical exercises, Jeanne helps us assume that childlikeness that pleases God and draws us near to his heart."

—Mary Beth Lagerborg
Author and Communications Manager
MOPS International (Mothers of Preschoolers)

"As a child in the foothills of the Mississippi Delta, my heart pounded with great anticipation when I heard Daddy's voice calling me in from the pasture to the dinner table. Jeanne Gowen Dennis has stirred within this grown woman's soul that same yearning to run to my heavenly Daddy's table to find solace from life's anguish, answers to life's questions, and peace amidst life's confusion. What a blessing to discover that I can once again become a child."

—Jill Rigby
Author of *Raising Respectful Children in a Disrespectful World*

"With personal examples, colorful metaphors, and biblical illustrations, Jeanne Gowen Dennis encourages us to nurture a tender, intimate relationship with God as our 'Abba, Daddy,' by seeing Him through the eyes of a child."

—Rebecca Barlow Jordan
Speaker and best-selling author, *40 Days in God's Presence*

"Seeing life through the eyes of a child brings one close to the heart of God. Seeing God through the eyes of a child brings one into His presence. *Running Barefoot on Holy Ground* does both! Highly recommended for anyone seeking an initial or deepened relationship with Jesus."

—Sherrie Eldridge
Author of *Twenty Things Adopted Kids Wish Their Adoptive Parents Knew*

"With refreshing insight, Jeanne Gowen Dennis inspires you to enjoy God with the abandon and innocence of a child. As you run in barefoot intimacy with Him, He'll set your soul free. . . . You'll discover holy ground beneath your feet, and you'll never wear shoes again!"

—Lynn D. Morrissey
Speaker and author of *Love Letters to God*

RUNNING *B*AREFOOT *on* HOLY GROUND

Childlike Intimacy with God

JEANNE GOWEN DENNIS

Kregel
Publications

Running Barefoot on Holy Ground: Childlike Intimacy with God

© 2006 by Jeanne Gowen Dennis

Published by Kregel Publications, a division of Kregel, Inc., P.O. Box 2607, Grand Rapids, MI 49501.

Library of Congress Cataloging-in-Publication Data
Dennis, Jeanne Gowen.
Running barefoot on holy ground: childlike intimacy with God / by Jeanne Gowen Dennis.
    p.   cm.
  Includes bibliographical references.
  1. Spiritual life—Christianity. 2. Spirituality. I. Title.
BV4501.3.D47   2006
248.4—dc22   2006008351

ISBN 0-8254-2488-7

Printed in the United States of America

06 07 08 09 10 / 5 4 3 2 1

For my earthly daddy, for your childlike faith;
and for Mom, for your steadfast love.

CONTENTS

𝒫REFACE

STANDING WITH THE REST OF THE CONGREGATION, I was listening to the praise music, but I just couldn't bring myself to participate. As I beat myself up mentally, I struggled with inadequacy. In three months I would be turning in the final manuscript for this book. As a Christian author and speaker, I felt that I should be living up to certain expectations—like participating in the praise singing and being glad to be in church worshipping the Lord—not feeling depression and loneliness as I stood alone in the pew while my husband sat in a plane heading for the Republic of the Congo.

Why did God give this writing assignment to me? I wondered. *Shouldn't this book's author be someone who's got it all together, a leader in the church, a woman everyone respects and loves?*

Then it hit me. God allowed me to write this book because I'm a regular person like you, a flawed person who knows the love of Jesus. I still go through doubt, temptation, fear, and pain. I get impatient, make mistakes, and embarrass myself on a regular basis. I know without a doubt that I need my heavenly Daddy's help to make it through each day. So please read this book as a letter from one imperfect child of God to another. Together we will discover what it means to know and love our Father and Creator with the simplicity of little children.

ᴀCKNOWLEDGMENTS

TAKING THIS BOOK FROM INSPIRATION TO COMPLETION was a long journey, made smoother through the encouragement and help of many others too numerous to mention by name. For those of you who have encouraged, advised, prayed, or simply listened, thank you. I would also like to express my heartfelt appreciation to all who allowed me to tell their stories or publish their writing in this book.

Dad and Mom, thank you for your example of faith and for helping me to understand through experience what a loving parent-child relationship is all about.

To my daughter, siblings, nieces and nephews, and all the children I've known and taught through the years, thank you for teaching me about childlikeness.

To my mother-in-law and Al, thank you for understanding when I've been busy.

To my critique groups, both the now-scattered Front Range Writers and my current group, thank you for trudging down the path with me through numerous drafts.

To my AWSA sisters, thank you for throwing me a lifeline on the lonely sea of writing.

To Sheila Seifert, Kathleen Groom, and Christine St. Jacques, thank you for reading and critiquing the final manuscript before submission. Your help was invaluable.

To Steve Barclift, Dennis Hillman, and everyone at Kregel Publications who believed in the vision and helped bring it to life. I am so grateful.

To my dear husband, Steve, thank you for always believing in me and supporting me, even when I doubted myself.

Most of all, I want to thank my Heavenly Daddy for loving me and daily drawing me closer to His heart. May He do the same for each and every reader.

$\mathcal{I}$NTRODUCTION

DO YOU EVER FEEL THAT LIFE IS RACING PAST WHILE you're just struggling to survive? As a Christian you know that God has a purpose for you, a reason for your existence beyond trying to make it through each week. You know there has to be more to life than what you're experiencing now. Think back to the day when you first believed, the moment when you knew that Jesus died for you so that you could have eternal life in Him. Wasn't it glorious to first know the Savior?

Does your soul long for that elation again? Do you yearn to let loose and run free like a new child of God enjoying your Daddy, the Eternal One? Perhaps you've forgotten how, or maybe you're so busy that you haven't had time to think about it lately. Trying to live a vibrant Christian life in an increasingly secularized culture sometimes feels like playing in a lighted London playground during a World War II nighttime air raid. We are continually bombarded with ungodliness from every side. The artillery of temptations and compromise stand ready to do their deadly work. Yet somehow in the midst of this we are expected to live joyfully in our heavenly Father's garden. But that's the secret. We're in *His* garden, and so we live under His protection.

In spite of the forces of evil fighting against us, we can live mostly stress-free lives every day of the week by nurturing a childlike relationship with God. In a culture where little that is sacred is held in awe anymore, we can still look to little children for examples of awe, wonder, faith, hope, and unconditional love. Jesus said that we must become like little children in order to enter God's kingdom (Matt. 18:3). God gave the secrets of eternal life to humble little children and hid them from the proud and wise (Matt. 11:25).

In this book, we will explore the characteristics of children that can help us learn to live in closer fellowship with God. Here you will find true stories, analogies, poetry, and hymns, as well as abundant Scripture to feed your soul. Because your life is busy, numerous verses of Scripture appear in the text and at the end of chapters so that you will not have to look them up. Memorize as many Scripture verses as you can. You will be amazed at how God will bring them to your mind just when you need them.

At the end of each chapter, exercises will help you practice childlikeness and draw closer to God. Some of the exercises may seem a bit strange. If they bother you, then skip them, but sometimes silly exercises help cement concepts in our minds.

Keep a journal as you go through the book, if you wish, and continue to keep it after you have finished reading. You might want to divide your journal into sections such as the following:

- My insights on childlikeness
- My insights on intimacy with God
- Things I discovered about God today
- My prayers and God's answers
- My favorite Scripture verses and why they spoke to me today
- Inspiring quotes and my reaction to them
- Activities I want to repeat and why
- Additional thoughts

You might want to go through this book as a fifteen-week study, either alone or with a group. No matter how you read it or how long you take, be open to the Holy Spirit and the work He wants to do in you.

Whatever you do with this book, may you find renewed joy and richer intimacy in your relationship with your eternal, almighty Daddy. Read it in the spirit of freedom instead of legalism. It is meant to be an adventure, just as our life in Christ is an adventure.

Now kick off your shoes, lay aside your adult inhibitions, and get ready for the elation of *running barefoot on holy ground.*

Part 1

IDENTIFICATION

$\mathcal{L}$OOK, DADDY!

Childlike Sight

> *To see a World in a Grain of Sand*
> *And a Heaven in a Wild Flower*
> *Hold Infinity in the Palm of your Hand*
> *And Eternity in an Hour*
> —WILLIAM BLAKE
> "AUGURIES OF INNOCENCE"

A WORLD IN A GRAIN OF SAND

It was a beautiful autumn day, and I needed some exercise. I wrapped my toddler daughter in a sweater, grabbed a light jacket, and started what I thought would be a walk around the block. Christine took off running, so I had to sprint to catch up with her. We had only reached the end of the driveway when she halted in front of me, bending to examine something on the ground. Anyone seeing the contortions I went through to keep from tripping over her would have nominated me for the clowns' hall of fame. What had piqued her interest? A rock. I almost suffered whiplash for a common little pebble.

After depositing the treasure in her pocket, Christine sped off again. *Good,* I thought. *Now I'll get some exercise.* She cut in front of me and stooped to the ground to watch a parade of ants march across the sidewalk. Giggling, she touched one of the insects with a tiny finger, then suddenly started running again.

Jogging behind my daughter, I savored the crisp air, entertaining the glorious feeling that we might actually make it past our next-door neighbor's house. Then I felt myself tripping over her. Sprawled on the grass, I watched her examine a dandelion like a doctor inspecting a wound. I sat up and continued to watch her. Suddenly she grabbed the stem in her fist and pulled it from the ground. She plopped on my lap, showing me the delicate petals of her latest discovery. Then she handed me the flower and started running again. After several similar incidents, we finally reached the third house from ours. I already felt as if I had worked out in a gym. I picked up Christine, turned her around, and aimed her in the direction of our house. It was mid-afternoon and I wanted to make it home before dark.

Eyes to See

Why do children notice so many things that adults miss? Maybe being closer to the ground gives them an advantage. Perhaps it's because they're discovering the wonders of the world around them for the first, second, or twentieth time, and somehow the novelty has not yet worn off. Unlike most adults, little children also pay attention to details. We are so distracted by our responsibilities that we often miss what is right before us. Perhaps we should take regular walks with toddlers and let them lead us along. Still, we'll only learn to see through their eyes if we use the time to exercise our sight, not just our bodies.

Simply having children around helps us learn to see again. One day my sister Christine and I were talking in the front yard of her home in Florida. I was holding her then two-year-old son, Tommy. Suddenly, he pointed to a sky filled with cotton-ball clouds and said, "Ay pane." I looked up. Not seeing anything but clouds, I said, "Yes, airplanes fly in the sky." He was insistent, pointing again. "Ay pane." Still seeing nothing, I repeated what I said before. With more excitement in his eyes, he tried to lift my chin to force me to look. *"Ay pane!"* Sure enough, there was a miniscule dot, hardly visible, above us. An airplane.

What has stolen our childlike powers of observation? Could it be that we fill up all our time, leaving no space for restful, quiet watching? What if my sister and I had spent five minutes outside in silence before our conversation, aware of each moment, observant of life's miracles unfolding before our eyes? I wonder what else we would have seen.

Every now and then, we do get it right, even if unintentionally. When I attended my first baseball game, I desperately wanted to witness a home run. Unfortunately, there were none. At the second game, I hoped again, and it happened. But I missed it. Instead of watching the field, I was marveling at God's greatness as a glorious pink and gold sunset played out over the stadium and the nearby Rocky Mountains. For about two seconds I was disappointed that I had missed seeing my first-ever home run. Then I realized that it was everyone else who had missed the most exciting event of the evening.

HEAVEN IN A WILDFLOWER

As we learn to open our eyes, we must also open our souls. Little children see with wonder, with curiosity, enthusiastic to absorb new information. Adults can experience this childlike wonder too. Isaac Newton described himself "like a boy playing on the seashore, and diverting myself in now and then finding a smoother pebble or a prettier shell than ordinary, whilst the great ocean of truth lay all undiscovered before me."

Marie Curie also referred to childlikeness as part of science: "A scientist in his laboratory is not only a technician: he is also a child placed before natural phenomena which impress him like a fairy tale."

Children express excited wonder whenever they make a new discovery. Perhaps that's why they're so close to God's heart. They seem to recognize the little messages He hid in creation for us—messages of His love and clues about His character.

The gospel of Mark tells us of a blind man Jesus healed in Bethsaida (8:22–26). After Jesus touched him, the man said that he could see people, but they looked like trees walking. When Jesus touched him again, he could see everything clearly. I think that we are often like that blind man. Somehow we don't quite get it, and we need another touch from the Creator to see what He has placed right before our eyes.

Writer and Bible teacher Cheryn Brewer recounts how God used His creation to speak to her for the first time:

> I had been a Christian for a few years and I couldn't understand how other people knew God was talking to them. He never talked to me and I was feeling like He didn't love me.
>
> I was thirty when I went to YWAM [Youth with a Mission] Discipleship Training School in the Los Angeles area. I had been there about a month when one day we were given an assignment to go off by ourselves and talk to God. I was to ask Him to tell me how much I meant to Him. My first thought was, "Oh sure, God isn't going to talk to me."
>
> I was wandering around outside for awhile then reluctantly said, "Okay God, I'm supposed to ask You, 'How much do I mean to You?'" Just as I asked that question, I bent down to pick up a tiny flower that was on the ground. (It was sweet alyssum, a ground cover that grows wild in Southern California. It has sprigs of tiny white or purple flowers with petals about the size of a flat pin head.)
>
> Just as I picked up that sprig of flowers, God spoke loud and clear to me. I knew it was God because He pushed every other thought out of my head and was very direct and said something I would never say to myself. He said, "Just as I would even think to create something that small is how much I care about every detail in your life."
>
> Boy, that blew me away! God spoke to me!
>
> That was about twenty years ago and I have since worked through many things that kept me from hearing God's voice in the early years. Now I have grown in my relationship with God and He speaks to me quite often. Yet that first time is the most meaningful to me, and I remember it like it was yesterday.[1]

Why *does* God care about every intimate detail of our lives, as He told Cheryn and demonstrates to us every day? Why are imperfect, self-ish humans so loved by Him? We are mere mortals who can't possibly understand God's motivation for creating us for intimacy with Him, but evidence of His love for us is all around us. He made His infinite loving-kindness clear to Cheryn through the tiny petals of a flower. How many of God's messages might we miss, just because we aren't paying attention?

INFINITY IN THE PALM OF YOUR HAND

To see as children see, all our senses must be alert. New worlds open up when children exercise their power of sight. They see with fresh eyes—fully, simply, and in intricate detail. Young children experience each new discovery to the fullest, first with their mouths, then with their hands and fingers, and finally with their whole beings. They "see" with all their senses and in every possible position: on their knees, on their stomachs, on their backs, upside down, backward, and side-ways. They explore the world with eyes wide open, closed, or squinted; through drinking glasses or cellophane; from inside cabinets, under coffee tables, and even in mirrors.

With a mirror, you can practice childlike sight without having to crawl on the ground or turn upside down (although you may want to do that too). Have you ever noticed how new and exciting familiar things become when viewed in a mirror? Just look at the reflection of your bedroom. It's still the room in which you spend almost one-third of your life, but the reflected image gives you a new perspective. It may look brighter, more peaceful, or even more cluttered than when you see it straight on. In some ways, the mirror image can be a truer one, because you're seeing the ordinary in a new way.

No wonder Lewis Carroll imagined his character Alice traveling through a looking glass! As she gazes into the mirror, she sees what she perceives as another world and entertains the possibility that the look-ing glass world could offer more excitement than her own.

When you were a child did you ever dream, like Alice, of passing through a looking glass to explore an exciting, imaginary world where everything is backward, yet somehow more wonderful than where you were? Did you ever try to draw, paint, or build those kingdoms that only existed on the other side of your imagination? Perhaps children pretend and dream because they instinctively sense the spiritual realm and know there must be someplace more wonderful than the world we inhabit. If we could only open our eyes and see as children see, we might venture beyond the mundane to the exhilarating.

ETERNITY IN AN HOUR

The apostle Paul compared our view of God to a view through a dull glass. We see inklings of His majesty and love through creation and in our lives, but our perception of God will not be perfect until we see Him face-to-face. Like Alice, we may see the images in our dull, earthly mirror as backward or distorted—especially when we experience pain and suffering—but the general impression should still leave us in awe of God's unfathomable greatness. Every now and then a clearer reflection jumps out at us. If we're paying attention, we can catch it and hold it in our hearts as a promise of greater understanding to come.

What messages has God communicated through your smoky looking glass? Try taking a walk with a little child. You won't get far, at least in distance covered. But you will travel deep into that world on the other side of the mirror as you begin to see more clearly the hand of God evident in simple things—like dandelions, pebbles, and wind. It's reflected in the sparkle of delight you'll see as that child touches a pill bug and watches it curl into a hard gray ball. Children can teach us to wonder again, to stand in awe of those incredibly complex creations that we have learned to take for granted. Even if you don't have a little child to guide you, try looking at the world as if you were seeing it for the first time.

One day, those of us who know our heavenly Father through faith in Jesus will pass from our backward world into heaven. The distortions in creation's mirror will disappear and we will see God clearly, face-to-face. Meanwhile, as we rediscover how to see a universe in a flower, a star, or a grain of sand, we can catch a glimpse of God's greatness and, like Alice, dream of a better world on the other side.

> *Immortal, invisible, God only wise,*
> *In light inaccessible hid from our eyes,*
> *Most blessed, most glorious, the Ancient of Days,*
> *Almighty, victorious, thy great name we praise.*
>
> —CHALMERS SMITH
> "IMMORTAL, INVISIBLE, GOD ONLY WISE"

CHILD'S PLAY

1. Go for a walk. Stop every two minutes and look around. What do you see? Pick up something ordinary like an acorn or a blade of grass. Examine it closely. What can you discover about its color, texture, or structure? What does that information tell you about its Creator?
2. Close your eyes and sit still. What do you hear? What do you smell? What do you feel? Do this exercise several days in a row and see if you notice more each day. Thank God for your senses.
3. Examine a familiar room or scene in a mirror. How does the mirror image look different? What do you see that you didn't notice before? What insights does this exercise give you about yourself? About God?
4. Go for a walk with a toddler and look at the world through his or her eyes. Notice the child's wonder, delight, and matter-of-fact acceptance of things as they are.
5. Observe the face of someone you love—every curve of the nose, every hue of the skin, each eyelash. Thank God for that person. Also thank Him for knowing you so well that He even numbers the hairs on your head (Matt. 10:30; Luke 12:7).
6. Eat a piece of fruit. Feel its texture, observe its structure, listen to the sound it makes as you unpeel it or bite into it. Savor each bite as if you had never tasted that food before. Glorify its Creator.

7. Observe little children and write down the qualities you would like to emulate. Then, focusing on one quality at a time, ask the Lord to help you grow in that area of childlikeness.

DADDY SAYS SO

About Children

At that time Jesus said, "I praise you, Father, Lord of heaven and earth, because you have hidden theses things from the wise and learned, and revealed them to little children."

—Matthew 11:25

And [Jesus] said: "I tell you the truth, unless you change and become like little children, you will never enter the kingdom of heaven."

—Matthew 18:3

"See that you do not look down on one of these little ones. For I tell you that their angels in heaven always see the face of my Father in heaven."

—Matthew 18:10

About Seeing and Understanding Him

But if from there you seek the LORD your God, you will find him if you look for him with all your heart and with all your soul.

—Deuteronomy 4:29

The heavens declare the glory of God;
      the skies proclaim the work of his hands.
Day after day they pour forth speech;
      night after night they display knowledge.
There is no speech or language
      where their voice is not heard.

Their voice goes out into all the earth,
   their words to the ends of the world.

           —Psalm 19:1–4

Taste and see that the LORD is good.

           —Psalm 34:8

He makes winds his messengers,
   flames of fire his servants.

           —Psalm 104:4

Seek the LORD while he may be found;
   call on him while he is near.

           —Isaiah 55:6

$\mathscr{P}$LAY WITH ME, DADDY!

Childlike Delight

I hear in the chamber above me
The patter of little feet,
The sound of a door that is opened,
And voices soft and sweet.

From my study I see in the lamplight,
Descending the broad hall stair,
Grave Alice, and laughing Allegra,
And Edith with golden hair.

A whisper, and then a silence:
Yet I know by their merry eyes
They are plotting and planning together
To take me by surprise.

A sudden rush from the stairway,
A sudden raid from the hall!
By three doors left unguarded
They enter my castle wall!

They climb up into my turret
    O'er the arms and back of my chair;
If I try to escape, they surround me;
    They seem to be everywhere.

They almost devour me with kisses,
    Their arms about me entwine,
Till I think of the Bishop of Bingen
    In his Mouse-Tower on the Rhine!

Do you think, O blue-eyed banditti,
    Because you have scaled the wall,
Such an old mustache as I am
    Is not a match for you all!

I have you fast in my fortress,
    And will not let you depart,
But put you down into the dungeon
    In the round-tower of my heart.

And there will I keep you forever,
    Yes, forever and a day,
Till the walls shall crumble to ruin,
    And moulder in dust away.
        —HENRY WADSWORTH LONGFELLOW
            "THE CHILDREN'S HOUR"

AT PLAY

Leo, Dan, and Daddy grunted, groaned, and laughed as they wrestled on the living room floor. It looked like a lot of fun.

"Can we play too?" Kathy and I asked.

"You're too little," Leo said.

"Wrestling isn't for girls," spouted Dan as he hit the carpet again.

Always the one to question boy-girl rules, I shot back, "Why not? We can do it." I didn't think it was fair for them to have so much fun with Daddy if we couldn't.

After the boys had played awhile, Daddy humored Kathy and me, letting us climb all over him and pretending that we were too much for his meager strength.

Years later, I watched my daughter playing with her daddy. She sat in her pajamas on a little cart like a princess, with her cape (her blanket) over her shoulders and her scepter (her stuffed skunk) across her arm. Steve pushed the cart around the circle of the living room, dining room, kitchen, and hall. Giggling, Christine called, "Faster, Daddy!"

Throughout her childhood, it was not uncommon for me to have a quiet moment of reflection suddenly interrupted by my screaming child streaking across the room chased by a growling bear. Or she might play a damsel in distress, and her daddy, in the character of a particular hero, would rescue her from some dire fate. Good daddies are lots of fun.

Have you ever played with your heavenly Daddy? No, I'm not suggesting that you wrestle on the floor with God, but as adults we need to learn how to enjoy playful times with Him—watching the antics of kittens, the twitching of a rabbit's nose, or the swaggering gait of a parade of ducks. It's in times such as these that we can become connoisseurs of the delights of daily life.

PRACTICING DELIGHT

For the third time in a day, I sent Christine to the corner for misbehaving. Ever since she had learned to assert her will, I had needed to expend more and more of my creative energy finding effective punishments for her. Sending her to sit in the corner was the most successful thing I had tried yet. Christine was such a social child that she dreaded having to sit alone facing the wall. I rejoiced that I had finally found something that worked—temporarily.

After a few minutes, her crying subsided and I heard her talking. I sneaked into the hallway to check on her. Through her vivid imagination, she was watching her own stories come alive as she traced their illustrations with her fingers across the blank screen of the wall. Like the literary character Pollyanna, Christine had learned to find something to be glad about, even during time-out.

Children find joy in little things, and they live out that joy to the fullest. Time moves slowly for them, perhaps because they know how to squeeze the maximum amount of living from each moment. Amid the stark realities of pain, death, and evil in this world, we could use a good dose of a child's imaginative delight, making room for joy when everything around us seems to be shutting it out.

"Delight yourself in the LORD and he will give you the desires of your heart," the psalmist instructs us (Ps. 37:4). But how can we do it? Life is tough, sometimes almost unbearable. Instead of escaping into work, activities, or entertainment, how can we keep a heavenly perspective and rejoice in each and every day (Ps. 118:24)?

The answer isn't in ethereal philosophies. It's in simple things like shiny pebbles by a gurgling stream, laughter, and love. Learning to delight again happens little by little as we learn to value the importance of a moment—and allow that moment to stretch into minutes as we discover polar bears in the clouds or we stop to watch a squirrel.

The older we get, the more we understand how precious time is—and the more we tend to waste it. My dad gave me a poignant example when I was visiting a few years ago. He spent several hours trying to make a decision about whether or not he should renew the maintenance agreements on his car and lawn tractor. That evening, Dad, who was eighty at the time, said, "I just realized that I wasted a day of my life."

The older he gets, the more aware Dad becomes of the short time he may have left. Although each day has become more precious to him, Dad never thinks that time spent stargazing, reading, laughing, playing, or praying—either alone or with his family—is wasted. And he's right.

How easily busyness takes over and squeezes delight out of our schedules! Do you ever get so busy that you only give half your attention to someone who is speaking to you? Our little daughter wouldn't tolerate that. When she detected that I wasn't giving her my full attention, she would climb on my lap, take my face in both her hands, and press her nose hard against mine. Then she talked, without loosening her grip. I couldn't help but listen!

How rich life could be if we would offer our undivided attention to each rose that scents our path, each bird that bequeaths a melody, and each child who reaches for our hands, instead of passing through life with our noses in newspapers, cell phones, computer monitors, and TVs.

TOGETHER TIME

Dad and I stood on the Flagler Beach, Florida, pier with the December sunshine on our backs. The wind played with my hair and with the waves. The pier rocked beneath us. Seagulls called. Fishermen cast their lines, and pelicans waited nearby to share whatever bounty the fishermen left behind.

We talked, not about anything of great significance, nothing earth-shattering or even memorable. Gazing over the side of the pier, I spotted our shadows. Beneath them, waves churned with spiderweb-like lines of light marbleizing their sea-green and blue hues. It reminded me of the fleetingness of life on earth and the vulnerability of the owners of those shadows. This moment etching itself into my memory cast only a faint shadow on the endless changeability of the sea, but it formed an indelible image for me—Daddy and his grown-up little girl, friends forever.

The truth about our lives and our relationships is more perceptible in the shadows, in the everyday little things, than in spotlighted events. It isn't so much what we do with our loved ones that matters. It's the time we spend together, paying attention and caring.

It's the same way with our relationship with God. Our time with Him is more important than anything else in our lives (see John 15:1–11). We need to enjoy Him in the company of others, as we do in church, but that can never replace the precious time spent in solitude with our Father and Creator, in our own secret place.

The Secret Place

Mom had dinner preparations well in hand. Kathy had charge of our younger siblings, and Maryland's crisp autumn air beckoned me. Growing up in a family of ten, my eleven-year-old heart often yearned for solitude. That day, as on countless other ones, I slipped out the back door and took the path into the woods beside our house. Winding my way past tulip poplars, pines, sycamores, and maples, I traipsed down the trail to a huge white oak tree—my tree. Warily, I studied the path and the woods in all directions to make sure no one saw me. Then I pulled myself onto the lowest branch and climbed into the thick crown where I was hidden from anyone searching from the ground.

I settled onto a stout bough and savored the woodland air. As I listened to the whispers of the rustling leaves that embraced me, I felt a peaceful presence in the wind, which I thought might be God. I could have sat there for hours, enjoying that sense of belonging. I was a world away from the buzz of family, school, and neighborhood activities, but close enough to the house that I could see and hear my mother when she called me from the side porch.

All too soon, the call came. I didn't answer, but immediately shimmied down the trunk and ran home. If I had answered, she might have seen me up there and it would have scared her. With three boys, two active girls, and two toddlers getting hurt all the time, she didn't need to worry about me too. Besides, if she had known where I was, my secret place wouldn't have been secret anymore.

I recently found out that my youngest sister felt the same need for solitude. Her retreat was a pine tree near the elementary school across the street from our house. Like me, she hid deep in the branches so that no one ever knew she was there.

The longing that my sister and I felt was not just an escape from living in a full house. I know now that it was a yearning to be alone with God, a time to let Him speak peace to our souls—a desire that dwells in every heart. Those of us who follow our heart's yearning and earnestly seek its fulfillment eventually find contentment through intimacy with God through Jesus. In the secret place of our hearts, we finally find our hiding place in Him as He becomes our place of comfort, understanding, and delight (Ps. 32:7).

DELIGHT IN ANTICIPATION

We were on the underground—the subway—on our way to Paddington Station in London when I noticed two British children and their parents with suitcases. The girl, who was about ten or eleven, prattled on in general good humor while her younger brother and parents listened, interjecting a few comments. Several moments of silence followed. Suddenly the girl's face sparkled. She bounced in her seat a little and pulled her suitcase higher on her lap. "I can't believe it!" she said. This happened several times. Apparently the family was going on holiday, connecting with the fast train to Heathrow Airport. Perhaps it was the children's first flight, or their first time to go to a dreamed-about destination. This little girl knew how to savor the anticipation of something thrilling.

If we truly believe God loves us, and if we trust with all our hearts that He will take care of our needs, then we can feel the same sort of thrill as we anticipate our future. Think of it! Living in constant companionship with the Lord in heaven will be wonderful beyond our wildest imaginings—and that delight can start right here and now. Just invite your heavenly Daddy to play with you.

> *Live while you live, the epicure would say,*
> *And seize the pleasures of the present day;*
> *Live while you live, the sacred preacher cries,*
> *And give to God each moment as it flies.*
> *Lord, in my views, let both united be;*
> *I live in pleasure when I live to Thee.*
> —PHILIP DODDRIDGE

CHILD'S PLAY

1. In 1 Thessalonians 5:17 Paul tells us never to stop praying. Set aside a day this week or month to practice "unceasing" prayer—living all day in continuous fellowship with God. Plan for His "visit" the same way you would for that of a dear friend or relative. On that day, cancel everything else so that you can spend all your time with Him. Welcome Him in. Take Him with you to your favorite spots, share with Him your fondest dreams, and eat a good meal with Him as your dinner companion. (Don't forget to thank Him for providing it.) Talk with Him. Share every feeling, disappointment, and victory. Several times during the day, take time just to listen to what He wants to speak into your spirit. If you do this, you'll probably remember the day as one of your best ever.

2. God's sense of humor is evident in many things He created. Visit a pet store or zoo and watch the antics of the animals, or read about some of the unusual-looking creatures God has made. Laugh with Him about them. He delights in His creatures, and we can delight with Him.

3. Have you ever noticed God's sense of humor in the unusual ways He sometimes answers our prayers? Try to remember some of those situations and write them down in your prayer journal. From now on, when you record anything humorous that God did, draw a happy face next to it. Then reread these stories when you need cheering up.

4. When you wake up in the morning for at least the next seven days, repeat Psalm 118:24, "This is the day the LORD has made; let us rejoice and be glad in it," and determine to rejoice no matter the circumstances. Then commit your day to the Lord—give it back to Him.

5. Practice delight. Find ten things today that you like or enjoy. Let the sense of delight fill your soul. Then praise God for each of those ten things.

6. Find a secret place to spend time with God. It could be in a small corner, in a closet, up a tree, behind a bush, somewhere in a church, or wherever you feel comfortable. Meet with Him there whenever you can and simply enjoy being together with the One who loves you best of all.

7. When you go to bed tonight, anticipate tomorrow. Even if it promises to be a rough day, think of something to look forward to. Examples:

   a. "I'm so excited that I will hear the robins sing tomorrow."
   b. "I'm grateful to drive to work tomorrow in the dependable car You've provided."
   c. "What a joy it will be to spend tomorrow with You, Lord!"
   d. "Thank You that I will not go to bed hungry."
   e. "Thank You that I have a voice to praise You."

DADDY SAYS SO

About Us Delighting in Him

> You will make known to me the path of life;
> In Your presence is fulness of joy;
> In Your right hand there are pleasures forever.
> —Psalm 16:11 NASB

> Delight yourself in the LORD
>   and he will give you the desires of your heart.
> —Psalm 37:4

> Direct me in the path of your commands,
>   for there I find delight.
> —Psalm 119:35

> When your words came, I ate them;
>   they were my joy and my heart's delight,

for I bear your name,
O LORD God Almighty.

—Jeremiah 15:16

About Him Delighting in Us

The LORD delights in those who fear him,
who put their hope in his unfailing love.

—Psalm 147:11

For the LORD takes delight in his people;
he crowns the humble with salvation.

—Psalm 149:4

The LORD your God is with you,
he is mighty to save.
He will take great delight in you,
he will quiet you with his love,
he will rejoice over you with singing.

—Zephaniah 3:17

$\mathcal{M}$Y DADDY TAKES CARE OF ME

Childlike Confidence

> Abba, I clutch Your hand as a tiny child
>   Who is learning to walk in Your light.
> My childish steps are so unsure.
>   Your loving arms keep me secure,
> And Your hand supports me when I start to fall.
>
> And in Your hand supporting me,
>   That mighty hand that calms the sea,
> I find compassion that gently soothes my fears.
>   As I clutch Your guiding hand,
> I see the Heart that understands
>   In scars of love upon Your hand supporting me.
>
> —JEANNE GOWEN DENNIS
> "YOUR HAND SUPPORTING ME"

CONFIDENCE IN DADDY'S ARMS

The rattling rush of sounds battled the blinding blur of sights as the train raced from London's Waterloo Station to Eton. The car in which we were riding was empty, save for our family and a couple with two young children sitting across the aisle from us. As the train rocked down the tracks, I noticed fearful blue eyes peering at us from behind the mother. I smiled. Suddenly, the eyes were gone, hidden in the mother's skirt. Then they turned away, staring out a window scratched with graffiti. Every few minutes the pigtailed child stopped tracing the etchings with her fingers and sneaked a glance at us. If she caught me looking at her, she quickly turned back to the window.

I went back to my reading, disappointed that I had not been able to connect with the little girl. Minutes later, the eyes appeared again, peeking from behind her father's shoulder. Finally, the child plopped into her father's lap. Having found a secure haven in her Daddy's arms, her sparkling eyes met mine, and she smiled. Soon little Fiona and I became friends.

No matter how strange and frightening the world appears, a child can face it boldly from the safety of a loving Daddy's arms. Like Fiona, we can find confidence, refuge, and rest from the stresses of life in our heavenly Daddy's arms.

HE GIVES US REST

The white and yellow curtains billowed toward my mother's back, and a gentle breeze carried the fresh scent of springtime. I hoped my mother wouldn't open her eyes and see that I was awake. If she thought my nap was over, I knew she would get up, and I just wanted to lie beside Mommy, watch the curtains, and enjoy the breeze. I was only three and didn't understand that I was enjoying the feeling of peace that comes from rest.

In contrast, my friend's son Jesse at age two disliked rest. He wanted to go, go, go, whether it was naptime or not. As long as Jesse moved, he would not fall asleep. His mother would hold his arms still, but then he would lift his legs. If she held his legs and arms, he would wiggle his body or head. Once, he even found a way to move his finger up and down to keep awake. When his mother stopped his finger from moving, Jesse immediately fell asleep, exhausted.

Many of us are like Jesse. We are so interested in life that we often deny ourselves rest. Exhausted, we continue moving as if rest were a punishment, not a provision. God loves us and knows that we do everything better when we have had our times of rest with Him. If we let Him, He will provide not only times and places for us to rest, but also everything else we need.

DADDY PROVIDES WHAT I NEED

A good father takes care of his family. Beth Lagerborg, publishing manager for MOPS (Mothers of Preschoolers) International, writes:

> My father was an honest, hard-working man whose mission in life was to provide for his family. He started a business at twenty-one and worked it until he died at sixty-three of a brief, intense battle with cancer. On our birthdays, each of us kids received from him as many silver dollars—as we got older as many crisp, new one dollar bills—as we were old (which he immediately whisked away and put into a savings account).
>
> My father died a month before my twenty-fifth birthday. When my mother cleaned out his dresser, she found an envelope containing twenty-five crisp one-dollar bills. On the front of the envelope were the words, "For Beth."
>
> I have saved one of those bills and kept it carefully folded in a compartment of my wallet where the boys won't find it and "borrow" it for lunch money! It reminds me of my father's love and provision for me.[1]

As the years passed, Beth found that her father's gift also reminded her of her heavenly Father's provision for her. Just as Beth's dad would never give her dog-eared bills, God gives only good gifts to His children as He provides for all their needs.

MY DADDY TAKES CARE OF ME

Whenever I came in from playing outside barefoot as a child, before I could cross the clean floor with my dirty feet, my mother would grab me and carry me upstairs to the bathroom. I would perch on the side of the tub while she sat on the closed toilet seat. She'd take one foot onto her lap and scrub it with warm, soapy water and a washcloth, and then do the other. Her hands soothed my battered feet as she removed all the dirt, grime, and grass stains left from the yards, sidewalks, and streets around our home. I always tried to make these cleanings last as long as possible, because in those moments I had Mommy all to myself. Her firm but tender touch made me feel secure and loved.

When God takes care of our needs, especially before we even ask, we feel the security of His love too. Author Karen Whiting recalls such a time in her daughter's life:

> Rebecca and I prayed before school everyday. On one particular day I received a call that she had bitten through her tongue in a fall and needed stitches immediately to stop the bleeding. However, we lived on a tiny island accessible only by boat or helicopter and without a resident surgeon. That week a dental convention was being held on the island and several dental surgeons were present, so Rebecca got the help she needed. Later she said that she knew God sent the doctor because we prayed for her safety that morning.[2]

Yes, a loving Daddy takes care of His children, not only when we have an emergency need, but also when we don't.

HE SHEDS HIS LIGHT

I was about seven years old when I first had a bedroom to myself. It was exciting to get into the big bed, but after Mom turned off the light and left the room, I suddenly felt alone. A faint glow from the street-light shone on the stained pine door leading to the hall and changed the door's swirled patterns into a monster's face. I tried to ignore it, but every time I opened my eyes, the monster glared menacingly back at me.

I couldn't bring myself to tell my parents why I was scared, but they knew I was. The next night, they gave me a nightlight and left the light on in the hall, which brought the door back into proper perspective. The light brought other comforts, as well. It gave me a sensation of warmth, as though gentle arms were holding me in the night.

Perhaps light comforts children not only because they can see things more clearly, but also because in it they experience a tiny bit of God's nature. Maybe that's one reason children can so readily love God. "God is Light, and in Him there is no darkness at all" (1 John 1:5 NASB). As Light, He dispels the darkness and casts out all our fear. Then His light envelops us, helping us to know that we belong to a Daddy who will protect us from harm.

DADDY WATCHES OVER ME

When my daughter was about ten, she was in a children's drama program. One Saturday they had a long rehearsal, and my husband and I were a little late picking her up. At first I wasn't concerned, because the director always held the children over for at least half an hour. We lived across town from the studio, and that day the traffic was especially bad. As the minutes ticked by, I began to worry. The studio was in a desolate part of town with nothing but fields and warehouses around it. By the time we pulled into the parking lot, it was empty—not a car in sight. I panicked. Where was my little girl?

Frantically, I ran to the entrance of the studio. I found my daughter pressed against the outside wall, trembling. The director had ended the rehearsal early and sent the children to play in a field across from the studio. When the other children had been picked up, the director left for an appointment. Christine saw her starting to leave. She raced and shouted after her, but the woman left anyway, either not knowing or not caring that one child was left alone.

When Christine told us about her ordeal, she said, "I was really scared, but I kept saying over and over, No evil will befall me [Ps. 91:10 NASB], and it didn't. God took care of me."

A little child trusts her daddy to take care of her. Unlike Christine's earthly daddy, who could not force his way through the traffic to reach her in time, our heavenly Daddy has the omnipotent power and unfailing love to take care of us in exactly the way we need, when we need it.

HE'LL BE THERE

When Jesse, the child who didn't like to rest, was eighteen months old, his family lived in an apartment complex with a pool. One day Jesse's dad lifted him out of the pool after taking him swimming and set him down on the edge of the cement deck.

"Stay here," said his dad. He pulled himself out of the pool to sit next to the boy and pulled a shirt over his own head. In the seconds it took to put the shirt on, Jesse disappeared. His father looked in the pool. Jesse, evidently confident that his dad would soon come to get him, stood calmly on the bottom, waiting.

That's the kind of confidence we can have in our heavenly Daddy. When we need Him, He is always there to take care of us.

FATHER TO THE FATHERLESS

Perhaps you have a hard time relating to all this talk about a daddy who takes care of you, because you never experienced this kind of care from a human father. Susan (name changed) knows how you feel, because God now stands in the void of what was missing in her youth—a sense of safety and security that she didn't have from her earthly parents. She recalls attending a retreat where a clip from the movie *The Horse Whisperer* was shown. In the scene, the injured horse bolted into a field, terrified. The horse whisperer followed the horse and then knelt in front of it. The man sat in silence with the animal for a whole day. Finally, the horse walked over and placed its head on the man's shoulder, in submission.

For Susan, God was like the horse whisperer, persistently following her and waiting with incredible patience. She says:

> It's like God's saying, "You're worth my time, and I will wait until you can bow in submission and place yourself in my care." God is trustworthy to wait for me to come to Him so that He can teach me how to be safe and whole and well. He has put me in places in my life where people and information guided me toward Him, even though I didn't get it growing up. I've discovered that God is the ultimate form of security, the security that can never fail, even when your earthly father lets you down.

Truly, our heavenly Daddy takes care of us. We can rest in the assurance that nothing is beyond His care—or His power.

> *Far away in the depths of my spirit tonight*
> *Rolls a melody sweeter than psalm;*
> *In celestial-like strains it unceasingly falls*
> *O'er my soul like an infinite calm.*
>
> *Peace! Peace! Wonderful peace,*
> *Coming down from the Father above;*
> *Sweep over my spirit forever, I pray,*
> *In fathomless billows of love.*
>   —W. D. CORNELL,
>   "WONDERFUL PEACE"

CHILD'S PLAY

1. Think about a place where you feel like you belong. Write down what makes you feel that way. Then think of the presence of God as a place even better than that.
2. Stop and rest with God. When you are at your busiest and most stressed, sit down, pick up the Bible, and ask God to speak to you through His Word. If you don't have a Bible with you, then ask

Him to bring an appropriate Scripture to mind. If none comes to mind, just be still and bask in His love for you.

3. Go into a closet or a room that is completely dark. Take your Bible and a flashlight. Sit on the floor and let the darkness sink in. Then turn on your flashlight and read about light in 1 John 1–2.

4. If you haven't been recording your prayers and God's answers, why not start keeping records today of how God answers your prayers? Then whenever you get discouraged, reread your accounts of how God provided for you and your loved ones. Make it a special time to reminisce with the Lord. Remember, He never changes (James 1:17).

5. Tonight before you go to sleep, say, "I will lie down and sleep in peace, for you alone, O LORD, make me dwell in safety" (Ps. 4:8). Choose to trust Him, and then enjoy your peaceful night's rest.

6. Sit in a dark closet. Is there a monster in your closet, something in the deepest corners of your soul that you're afraid to confront, afraid to talk about even to God? He knows. Talk to Him about it. Don't be afraid. Let Him take care of it. Then turn on the closet light as a sign to remind you that God casts His light into the darkest shadows and replaces the gloom with clean, glorious radiance.

7. Read some Bible verses that talk about waiting on God, such as Psalms 27:14; 33:20; 37:7; 38:15; 119:166; 130:5; Proverbs 20:22; Isaiah 30:18; and Micah 7:7. Then whatever your need, remember to stand like little Jesse, and just wait for your heavenly Daddy to come.

DADDY SAYS SO

About Confidence in God

> The LORD is my light and my salvation—
> whom shall I fear?

The LORD is the stronghold of my life—
of whom shall I be afraid?
When evil men advance against me
to devour my flesh,
when my enemies and my foes attack me,
they will stumble and fall.
Though an army besiege me,
my heart will not fear;
though war break out against me,
even then will I be confident.

—Psalm 27:1–3

About God's Provision, Care, and Protection

You are my hiding place;
you will protect me from trouble
and surround me with songs of deliverance.

—Psalm 32:7

When I am afraid,
I will trust in you.

—Psalm 56:3

There is surely a future hope for you,
and your hope will not be cut off.

—Proverbs 23:18

"For I know the plans I have for you," declares the LORD, "plans to prosper you and not to harm you, plans to give you hope and a future."

—Jeremiah 29:11

But the Lord is faithful, and he will strengthen and protect you from the evil one.

—2 Thessalonians 3:3

Every good and perfect gift is from above, coming down from the Father of the heavenly lights, who does not change like shifting shadows.

—James 1:17

Cast all your anxiety on him because he cares for you.

—1 Peter 5:7

About Rest

I will lie down and sleep in peace,
 for you alone, O LORD,
 make me dwell in safety.

—Psalm 4:8

Find rest, O my soul, in God alone;
 my hope comes from him.

—Psalm 62:5

He who dwells in the shelter of the Most High
 will rest in the shadow of the Almighty.

—Psalm 91:1

Be at rest once more, O my soul,
 for the LORD has been good to you.

—Psalm 116:7

In vain you rise early
 and stay up late,
toiling for food to eat—
 for he grants sleep to those he loves.

—Psalm 127:2

Come to me, all you who are weary and burdened, and I will give you rest.

—Matthew 11:28

$\mathcal{M}$Y DADDY CAN DO ANYTHING

Childlike Amazement

Today I want to praise Him, but the day
Itself is praising Him more fully than
These words of mine. Each bird-call says His name;
The hills stand tall to shout His majesty;
The waters flow out His foreverness;
The winds insist that trees applaud; and I
Stand mute before such vast articulation.

Since my voice will be lost in such a choir,
My little walk-on role unnoticed in
The drama of eternal reverence,
I wonder if He needs my words at all.
Perhaps as I stand breathlessly and hear
Creation celebrate His name, He hears
My soft "Amen" and takes it for a psalm.[1]

—LOIS B. EADES
"MY PSALM"

My Daddy's the Best

"No, our daddy's the best one of all," I said, arguing with a group of neighborhood kids. "*Our* daddy can do anything!" my sister Kathy added. As we tried to convince them of our father's obvious superiority, the other children took turns giving examples of the incredible feats their dads had accomplished.

"My dad can climb on the roof," one boy said.

"Mine can do that too—and with only one hand," I countered.

"But my dad knows how to tell the best stories in the world," said a girl.

Kathy and I smiled knowingly at each other. We had them now. "No, our dad tells the funniest stories," she said. "He makes up new ones every night about our stuffed animals."

"You ought to hear the ones about my stuffed tiger," I added. "Dad and I are in the jungle and there's danger all around us. Suddenly, a tiger jumps out and scares us. But then we find out he's a nice tiger who wants to be our friend. And at night he shrinks down into a soft stuffed animal and sleeps with me."

We almost had them until one girl ended the argument with, "My dad fought in the war. He helped stop a bad man named Hitler and saved lots of people's lives. He even won a medal."

Everyone fell silent. Our dad didn't fight in World War II, so Kathy and I couldn't top that one. We trudged home feeling like traitors because we had not been able to convince the other children that our dad really was the best. In our hearts we knew he was. We just didn't know how to prove it to anyone else.

I've had the same struggle in my quest to help others know how incredibly wonderful my heavenly Daddy is. Even though His greatness is far beyond anything we could imagine, greater than all the earthly daddies who ever lived put together, many people don't believe it. In fact, for a long while, I didn't believe it myself.

Duped?

Some of my professors had convinced me that the Bible was only mythology, and I felt it was my duty to convince my mother to agree with me. We stood in the kitchen arguing.

"No, Mom, Moses led the Israelites across the Red Sea during a drought. Then a flash flood came and killed the Egyptians. And Jesus must have been on a sandbar or an ice floe when He walked on water." I explained everything according to the laws of nature. My new philosophy left no room for miracles.

Wringing her hands, Mom tried to reason with me on the basis of Scripture, but I had been persuaded that she was misinformed and naive. I couldn't help feeling sorry for her. I was sure she'd been duped. When she turned to the subject of creation, I knew I had her.

"Everything came about by evolution," I explained. "It happened slowly over billions of years." I used the arguments and scientific jargon I had learned at college, trying to persuade her to my viewpoint. I pounded her with all my "proofs" until she backed down. Seeing the pain in her face, I softened the blow a little. "If evolution is how everything developed, then that must be the way God decided to create everything." It was my way of compromising, but even as I said the words, I wondered if God had anything to do with it at all. I had begun to believe that we had all been lied to about God, that He was something other than what I had been taught all my life.

From that point, I made the short journey to accepting other philosophies. As an impressionable college student in the early 1970s, I joined my peers in thinking that I should shop around and choose the religion that best fit my intelligence and temperament. There were many options, but some were a bit too weird for my taste. Eventually, I did reject the God of the Bible for a transcendental god that was in everything. The romantic notion that I could rise to higher spiritual levels drew me in, even though I was uncomfortable with the idea of ultimately becoming one with the universe. Losing my identity in a cosmic soup scared me. Still, reincarnation made sense to the fantasy lover in me, and I enjoyed daydreaming about what I might have been in past lives.

LOVE CALLING

For several years, I was content in my intellectual snobbery. I thought I could make my own decisions and live the way I wanted to. Then, when I was in my late twenties, my husband, Steve, and I had a daughter. Suddenly, what I believed became more important. I needed to know what to teach her, and I wanted it to be the truth, so I began to search for truth in earnest. When two friends heard that I was looking, they each invited me to visit their respective churches. The next Sunday I visited both. In the morning, I sat in a circle with about fifteen people (the whole "church") as they discussed whether there was sound in the forest when a tree fell with no one to hear it. I wanted to like this place and these people, but something essential was missing. I soon realized that they didn't have the answers. They didn't even have the questions. Like me, they were still searching.

At the other church's evening service, they talked about Jesus. Most of it went over my head. It sounded preachy and I didn't like it, but I enjoyed the music. One line from a song penetrated my heart, because it told me that God could understand my confusion.[2] *My confusion.* Yes, I was confused, and I felt a glimmer of hope that there could be a God who understood. Driving home that night, I felt a Presence with me. I know now that it was the Holy Spirit, drawing me to Himself.

At home, Steve asked me how I liked the service. I amazed myself by saying, "I didn't, but I'm going back." After a few weeks, I decided that Jesus was the One I had been searching for, but I still had a long way to go before being convinced that the Bible was completely true. Arrogantly, I judged whether less "enlightened" people than I were taking its accounts too literally. My journey back to faith and trust in God would be a long one with many twists and turns—but I found a few clear signposts along the way.

SUCH VAST ARTICULATION

Have you ever seen the stars away from city lights? Living in a large city like Denver, I seldom have the opportunity to see the sky filled with stars, because the city lights obscure them. But one time—only once—I caught a glimpse of what God showed Abraham when He promised that his descendants would be as many as the stars in the heavens.[3]

Steve, Christine, and I were camping in the mountains of Wyoming, far away from any city. I had just gone into the tent to snuggle into my sleeping bag when Steve whispered, "Come out here! Quick! You need to see this."

"It's not a wild animal, is it?" I imagined him out there watching a bear or a mountain lion, and I didn't want any part of it.

"Just come out here."

I crept out slowly, ready to dive back in if necessary. Steve pointed upward, and I gazed at ebony velvet, sprinkled with fiery diamonds and diamond dust so thick that it almost overcame the darkness. "I think it's the Milky Way," he said. Shivering in the fir-scented night, I caught a glimpse of God's majesty and heard the stars singing His praises. And I knew without a doubt that God, a being far and above anything the human mind can fathom, created every one of them. I simply knew it.

From then on I became an observer of nature. Even though I had studied botany and horticulture in college, I would wonder as I fingered the delicately-veined petals of a rose what intricate workings opened the blossom, nourished the petals, and perfumed the air. Could chance mutations, even with the help of natural selection over billions of years, bring about the beauty, order, and diversity I saw? Science attempted to explain it. Evolution claimed the credit. But with the evidence in my hand, I knew that chance was too clumsy an inventor to have fashioned a rose petal, let alone a rose. In the end, I made the conscious choice to put my faith in what God revealed instead of what humans theorized and "discovered." I was finally able to see the Creator—away from "city lights"—and I knew the Bible was true.

BLINDING LIGHTS

What "city lights" blind us from seeing our Creator? Why are many scientists, especially, unable to see the evidence that God has made so clear? Of all people, they should be the most easily convinced. Yet, even as they express amazement at nature's beauty, order, and complexity, many of them miss seeing the reflections of the Creator that are right before their eyes. Could it be they are blindly accepting academia's formal position, refusing to open their eyes, or standing too close to see clearly?

According to Scripture, only God's gift of faith can open our eyes:

> By faith we understand that the worlds were prepared by the word of God, so that what is seen was not made out of things which are visible. (Heb. 11:3 NASB)

Those who do not have faith in God do not have the Holy Spirit to help them understand the truth.

> The man without the Spirit does not accept the things that come from the Spirit of God, for they are foolishness to him, and he cannot understand them, because they are spiritually discerned. (1 Cor. 2:14)

Yet all of us are responsible for the knowledge we have. When we begin to understand the intricate workings of the natural world, our instinctive response is wonder and awe. We know it all came from somewhere, but where? Our postmodern culture refuses to give credit to God. The impersonal theory of evolution demands nothing from us. If we came to this earth by chance, then we can live as we please and answer to no one but ourselves. Tragically, the scientific community at large credits the theory of evolution with anything it cannot explain, and evolution has become the god of postmodern science.

Regardless of what we learned in science classes, we all know the truth, whether or not we will admit it to ourselves. Every human being understands, at least in some small way, that God exists. We know because God has shown us:

> For the wrath of God is revealed from heaven against all ungodliness and unrighteousness of men who suppress the truth in unrighteousness, because that which is known about God is evident within them; for God made it evident to them. For since the creation of the world His invisible attributes, His eternal power and divine nature, have been clearly seen, being understood through what has been made, so that they are without excuse. (Rom. 1:18–20 NASB)

REVELATION

One sunny afternoon I joined my daughter and two of her friends on what we expected to be a quest for information. Sitting at the kitchen table, the girls and I examined an interior decorated in sunny shades of avocado green, creamy orange, and freshwater-pearl white. It was a perfect blend of art and utility, an exquisite masterpiece of beauty and engineering. Together we marveled at the skill it must have required to put together this wonder—the crayfish we were dissecting.

Have you ever been surprised, as we were, to find beauty in unexpected places? Loveliness in nature shouts of God, because beauty makes no sense without the Creator. After all, what purpose does beauty serve? It can bring joy, peace, amazement, and contentment, but these too are intangibles. Science cannot possibly explain the reasons for beauty's existence, and no creatures benefit from its resulting intangibles as much as humans do. Nature's beauty is a gift from God to His creatures, as well as a faint but discernible reflection of Himself.

God made stars so numerous that they cannot be counted. He made wind, waves, rose petals, and the rosebud cheeks of our children. If He can do that, then our Daddy can do much more than we could ever imagine. He's the only Daddy who really can do anything. He's the best Daddy of all.

I sing th'almighty power of God that made the mountains rise,
That spread the flowing seas abroad, and built the lofty skies.
I sing the wisdom that ordained the sun to rule the day;
The moon shines full at God's command, and all the stars obey.

I sing the goodness of the Lord, who filled the earth with food,
Who formed the creatures through the Word, and then pronounced them good.
Lord, how Thy wonders are displayed, where'er I turn my eye,
If I survey the ground I tread, or gaze upon the sky.

There's not a plant or flower below, but makes Thy glories known,
And clouds arise, and tempests blow, by order from Thy throne;
While all that borrows life from Thee is ever in Thy care;
And everywhere that we can be, Thou, God art present there.

—ISAAC WATTS
"I SING TH' ALMIGHTY POWER OF GOD"

CHILD'S PLAY

1. Run your hands through water and marvel at how precious and wonderful it is. Then wonder at the miracles Jesus did with water. He walked on it, calmed a raging sea, and turned water into wine. He promises us living water so that we will never thirst. Take a drink of water to quench your physical thirst. Now take a drink of Living Water by spending time in God's Word.

2. Pick up a seed. Finger it. Examine it. Then look at the life that can come from that seed. Observe the flower, bush, or tree that it can produce. Imagine the hundreds of other plants and seeds that can be produced through successive generations. Better yet, plant the seed and watch it grow. Then wonder at God's greatness and creativity.

3. Who sowed the seed of God's truth in you? If the person is still living, write or call to thank him or her for introducing you to Jesus. Better yet, buy the person a beautiful plant, bush, or tree and

explain that it is symbolic of your life in Christ, a new life that began because he or she cared enough to tell you about Him.

4. Watch a cut heal. It is a miracle taking place before your eyes. Give God the glory due Him for creating us, for we are "fearfully and wonderfully made" (Ps. 139:14).

5. Read Genesis 1 and John 1. God said that He created. He said it over and over. God means what He says. So whom will you believe, God or people?

6. Go on a treasure hunt, exploring the wonders of creation. Try to catch a glimpse of God's footprints in the grass, discover His fingerprints on a tree trunk, and hear His voice in the breeze. In other words, try to find out more about God by observing what He made. Write down your observations.

7. Look at the night sky. What do you see? If you see a myriad of amazing creations, how does that sight make you feel about God? Sing about it. Use a hymn such as "How Great Thou Art" or make up one of your own.

DADDY SAYS SO

About God as Creator

> So God created man in his own image,
> in the image of God he created him;
> male and female he created them.
>
> —Genesis 1:27

> When I consider your heavens,
> the work of your fingers,
> the moon and the stars,
> which you have set in place,
> what is man that you are mindful of him,
> the son of man that you care for him?
>
> —Psalm 8:3–4

By the word of the LORD were the heavens made,
their starry host by the breath of his mouth.
He gathers the waters of the sea into jars;
he puts the deep into storehouses.
Let all the earth fear the LORD;
let all the people of the world revere him.

—Psalm 33:6–8

For you created my inmost being;
you knit me together in my mother's womb.

—Psalm 139:13

"To whom will you compare me?
Or who is my equal?" says the Holy One.
Lift your eyes and look to the heavens:
Who created all these?
He who brings out the starry host one by one,
and calls them each by name.
Because of his great power and mighty strength,
not one of them is missing.

—Isaiah 40:25–26

This is what God the LORD says—
he who created the heavens and stretched them out,
who spread out the earth and all that comes out of it,
who gives breath to its people,
and life to those who walk on it.

—Isaiah 42:5

Yet, O LORD, you are our Father.
We are the clay, you are the potter;
we are all the work of your hand.

—Isaiah 64:8

This is what the LORD says:
"Heaven is my throne,
  and the earth is my footstool.
Where is the house you will build for me?
  Where will my resting place be?
Has not my hand made all these things,
  and so they came into being?"
  declares the LORD.
"This is the one I esteem:
  he who is humble and contrite in spirit,
  and trembles at my word."

—Isaiah 66:1–2

About God's Power

In his hand is the life of every creature
and the breath of all mankind.

—Job 12:10

For in him we live and move and have our being.

—Acts 17:28

I pray also that the eyes of your heart may be enlightened in order that you may know the hope to which he has called you, the
riches of his glorious inheritance in the saints, and his incompara-
bly great power for us who believe. That power is like the working
of his mighty strength, which he exerted in Christ when he raised
him from the dead and seated him at his right hand in the heavenly
realms, far above all rule and authority, power and dominion, and
every title that can be given, not only in the present age but also in
the one to come.

—Ephesians 1:18–21

$\mathcal{T}$HAT'S *MY* DADDY!

Childlike Ownership

My Jesus, I love Thee, I know Thou art mine
For Thee all the follies of sin I resign
My gracious Redeemer, my Savior art Thou
If ever I loved Thee, my Jesus, 'tis now.
—WILLIAM R. FEATHERSTON
"MY JESUS I LOVE THEE"

TRULY MINE

My sister Kathy and I were talking on the phone, discussing her young twins, Pam and John. "John seems to be artistic, and I think Pam got some musical talent from Mom," Kathy said.

"I'm sure John inherited his artistic talent from you," I added.

This line of conversation continued until we both realized what we were saying and burst out laughing. We had forgotten that Pam and John had been adopted. In our minds and hearts, John and Pam are our blood relatives.

Believers in Jesus become God's true children, just as Pam and John are truly part of our family. And as God's children, we can run to Him just as any child runs to his or her father.

ON DADDY'S LAP

"Make room for me!" Marie cried, scrambling up onto the easy chair to join us. Poor Dad! He was being crushed by several of his children as we vied for space on his lap. He oomphed and groaned, but somehow managed to fit us all. In Dad's lap we found stories about growing up long ago when Daddy was small like us, when only wealthy families owned automobiles and green streetcars ruled the road in his native Washington, D.C. We were fascinated to hear about people who knew how to make homemade sausage, root beer, and ice cream, and about how Dad and his brothers played baseball in the back alley with the neighborhood boys. All of us kids knew we owned a spot on Dad's lap—a place of comfort, warmth, and belonging, a throne where each daughter was a princess, and each son, a prince.

But then suddenly one day, I felt oversized and awkward sitting on Dad's lap. I didn't fit anymore. Feeling like a deposed princess, I stepped aside as the littler kids took over the realm. Suddenly, in a place I had always counted on, I no longer belonged.

I remember with my own daughter how heartsick I felt when I realized that she was outgrowing my lap. As a parent, I wanted to be able to hold her, both to show my love and to comfort her whenever her world turned complex, frightening, or painful. I wanted her to have a place of safety and consolation that she could count on, but I realized that neither her dad nor I could provide a permanent haven for her. At some point, our laps would become too small and she would have to climb on her heavenly Daddy's lap, a place where she would always belong.

BELONGING

We each need to feel that there is someplace where we belong. Author Janet Holm McHenry recalls a special place from her childhood:

One of my greatest memories as a child was twirling my way through the revolving front doors of Marsh's Department Store in Hudson, New York, where my dad was assistant manager. . . . I felt as though I were the princess sweeping into the presence of the king.

All the middle aged ladies loved my dad and would come up to me right away to let me know where he was in the four-story building. Once I'd find Dad, he'd give me a dime and I'd go into the employees' room, open the refrigerator, and put my dime in the cup. That would buy a bottle of Coca Cola and a package of cheese and peanut butter crackers. It was the best possible way to spend my afternoons after school.[1]

As children of our heavenly Father, the Manager of the universe, we belong wherever He is. The more we seek Him out and spend time with Him, the better we will recognize His voice, especially when He calls our names.

RECOGNIZING THE BELOVED'S VOICE

At about twelve years old, I was doing homework in the bedroom I shared with my sister Kathy when I heard a muffled voice calling me by the name my family used at home. "Jeanne Aaaaan! Jeanne Aaaaaan!"

The voice sounded angry, and at first I thought it was my dad. Rather than answer that slightly familiar tone, I followed the sound cautiously to the laundry room. Laughing eyes met mine. My brother Leo chuckled from behind the T-shirt he had used to muffle his words.

"You thought you were in trouble, didn't you?"

I rolled my eyes with a shake of my head.

He laughed again. "I almost had you fooled, didn't I?"

Almost, but not quite. I knew the sound of my daddy's voice. Sometimes when Dad called, he sounded angry. That's when I knew I *was* in trouble. Other times his voice sounded calm, anxious, earnest, or joyful, depending on the situation. Regardless, it always sounded exactly like Dad.

Jesus said that His sheep know His voice and will not follow another (John 10:1–5, 27). We can't physically hear Him speaking, but if we are His, we can recognize God's still, small voice (1 Kings 19:11–12). Just as with our earthly fathers, our heavenly Father's voice may speak to reprimand or correct us. God may assign us a task, comfort us, teach us a lesson, or let us know that He's pleased with us. No matter what else He says, He always calls us to draw nearer to Him, and He, in turn, draws nearer to us (James 4:8).

When Steve and I were dating, my heart thrilled every time I heard him say my name. The phone had a more melodic ring when he was calling, and I never wanted to hang up. As soon as he spoke a word, I knew his voice, and its sound went straight into my heart. That's the way it is with true love. Hearts immediately connect at the sound of the beloved's voice.

To those of us who know God, the voice of our Most Beloved fills us with joy as He imparts to us the secrets of His heart.

IT'S A SECRET!

We had just finished dinner, and my mentally disabled brother, Tim, called me out of the dining room into the kitchen.

"We need to be quiet. It's a secret," he said. It was getting close to his birthday, so I suspected the reason for his secret.

"This year I would like football players on my cake."

"Okay, Tim, I'll see what I can do."

"Don't tell anyone I told you. You know. It might spoil the surprise."

I promised to keep his secret safe. Every year it was the same thing. My brother trusted only me with his birthday cake preference so that everyone else would think he was surprised when he got to see what kind of sports figures were on his cake. I felt that I had been entrusted with a precious treasure, and I tried to handle it carefully.

Children like to tell secrets. Although even silly secrets invite a closer relationship, a child's true confidences bestow honor and trust and welcome the listener into the child's inner circle. My sister Christine received such a treasure one day when her son Joey climbed on her lap and said, "I want to tell you a secret." Then he cupped his hands over her ear and whispered, "Mommy, you're my best friend."

As believers, we have been invited into God's circle of intimates. He takes us into His confidence as His Holy Spirit guides us in understanding the secrets of faith (John 16:13–15; 1 Cor. 2:14). Likewise, our relationship with Him and our sense of belonging to Him grow as we make Him our confidante. God understands us thoroughly. He already knows what we're thinking, just as I knew what my brother's request would be, but our intimacy with our heavenly Daddy deepens as we candidly share the secrets of our hearts.

Do you trust God with all your secrets, all your deepest thoughts and desires? If not, what is holding you back? Are you afraid He'll let you down, ask too much of you, or condemn you for your honest feelings? Perhaps you're not quite ready to trust God so completely. Or maybe you've walled up your heart and thrown away the key.

THE SECRET GARDEN

Rumors of a locked garden kept hidden for years intrigued Mary Lennox. The garden was the first thing to pique her interest after her parents died and she was forced to move from India to the moors of northern England to live with her strange uncle.

Where was this garden? Why would someone lock it up? Mary was determined to find not only the garden but also the secrets it hid. First she found the key, then the gate. Inside she discovered what appeared to be a dead mass of chaos. When she let a new friend into the secret, he taught her how to weed and prune to give the growing things air and space. Soon they let another child into the secret, Mary's spoiled invalid cousin, Colin. As the children took ownership of the abandoned garden and brought it back to life, the solid walls around Mary's and Colin's hearts crumbled to ruins, and for the first time joy blossomed inside.

Frances Hodgson Burnett's book *The Secret Garden* paints a literary picture of the self-destructive methods we often use to suppress painful memories and protect ourselves from further pain. Like the children in the story, we need to unlock the door to the walls we've built around our hearts, work the soil, pull out the weeds, and let in the fresh air so our souls can bloom again.

If there is a walled, locked-up place in your heart, try to figure out why. Did you lock it because you were hurt or betrayed by someone you trusted and you couldn't stand the memory of it? Perhaps you feared being hurt again. You may doubt it now, but somewhere inside you the flowers are still there, ready to be weeded and tended. Your best Friend, your Daddy, your Beloved, is waiting to meet you inside those walls. Together you can work the soil to give the roots room to spread. You can cut off the dead wood to allow air and sunshine in, prune the good branches to stimulate new growth, and open the gates to let the breezes flow freely. Then you will bloom again, and you can enjoy the restored garden of your soul with your beloved Daddy by your side.

Perhaps this process sounds too simplistic. Do your wounds run deep? Intense pain that has festered over time doesn't readily heal without help.

FREE AGAIN

A few years ago, I suffered with a frozen shoulder, a condition that kept me from moving my arm past a 30-degree angle. In order to get the joint loosened, I endured weeks of physical therapy and exercised my arm and shoulder several times per day. Moving my arm even a quarter of an inch past its frozen position was excruciating, and I couldn't have done it alone. My physical therapist had me work with machines, weights, and elastic therapy bands to aid the process. When I couldn't force myself to move my arm any further, a therapy band or weight would finish the process for me. At the end of each session the therapist applied moist heat and manually worked my shoulder and arm. Each week I could move a little more until finally my mobility came back and the pain left.

Healing emotional pain can be even more excruciating than a frozen shoulder—and take more time to heal. You may have to work through whatever you're dealing with gradually, and you may need help from books, support groups, or a professional Christian counselor or pastor. Don't give up. Press on through the pain. Let the Holy Spirit be your "therapy band," pulling your frozen soul looser and looser each hour, each day, until you can trust again. Finally, you will be free to love and be loved. Then you will know that you belong to your heavenly Daddy, and He belongs to you.

> *O might I hear Thy heav'nly tongue*
> *But whisper, "Thou art mine!"*
> *Those gentle words shall raise my song*
> *To notes almost divine.*
>
> —ISAAC WATTS
> "BEGIN, MY TONGUE,
> SOME HEAVENLY THEME"

CHILD'S PLAY

1. Adoption is like grafting. Just as a grafted branch or bud becomes part of the vine or tree, an adopted child becomes a true part of the family. When we accept Jesus as Lord and Savior, we are grafted into Him and are adopted as God's children. Go to an orchard, a vineyard, or a nursery and observe some plants that have been grafted. Thank God for this amazing natural phenomenon that helps us understand our adoption into His family.

2. Heaven is the ultimate place of belonging for those who believe in Jesus. Read about it in Revelation 21:1–22:6.

3. Do you recognize God's voice when He speaks to you? What is it about His voice that is unique? Discuss this topic with Christian friends and find Scripture to support your views.

4. Tell the Lord the deepest secrets of your heart, knowing that He loves you just as you are. Pour out your feelings to Him and listen for His response.

5. Find a patch of lawn or garden that needs cleaning out, and invite the Lord to help you purge the weeds in your heart as you weed the garden. When you pull a physical weed, call it a name, such as

unforgiveness, anger, frustration, resentment, jealousy, or gossip. Ask the Lord to help you overcome that problem in His strength and help you tend the flowers of love, joy, peace, patience, and the other fruit of the Spirit (Gal. 5:22–23).

6. Call up two Christian friends and encourage them in their faith. Talk honestly about something you have seen in them that reminds you of Jesus. Encourage them to keep it up and promise to pray for them. When you get off the phone, keep your promise and pray.

7. Ephesians 5:25 discusses Jesus' love for His church in terms of a husband's love for his wife. The church is also referred to as Jesus' bride in John 3:29 and in Revelation 19:7 and 21:9. As a believer, you are part of the bride of Christ. Rejoice in His love, tell Him He's your best Friend, and listen for His whisper saying, "You are Mine!"

DADDY SAYS SO

About Belonging to God

> Know that the LORD is God.
> It is he who made us, and we are his;
> we are his people, the sheep of his pasture.
>
> —Psalm 100:3

> Fear not, for I have redeemed you;
> I have summoned you by name; you are mine.
>
> —Isaiah 43:1

He calls his own sheep by name and leads them out. When he has brought out all his own, he goes on ahead of them, and his sheep follow him because they know his voice. But they will never follow a stranger; in fact, they will run away from him because they do not recognize a stranger's voice.

> —John 10:3–5

I am the good shepherd; I know my sheep and my sheep know me.

—John 10:14

If you belonged to the world, it would love you as its own. As it is, you do not belong to the world, but I have chosen you out of the world. That is why the world hates you.

—John 15:19

And you also are among those who are called to belong to Jesus Christ.

—Romans 1:6

But he who unites himself with the Lord is one with him in spirit.

—1 Corinthians 6:17

But when the completion of the time came, God sent His Son, born of a woman, born under the law, to redeem those under the law, so that we might receive adoption as sons. And because you are sons, God has sent the Spirit of His Son into our hearts, crying, *"Abba,* Father!"* So you are no longer a slave, but a son; and if a son, then an heir through God.

—Galatians 4:4–7 HCSB

He predestined us to be adopted through Jesus Christ for Himself, according to His favor and will.

—Ephesians 1:5 HCSB

About Confiding in God

> In my distress I called to the LORD;
> I called out to my God.
> From his temple he heard my voice;
> my cry came to his ears.

—2 Samuel 22:7

The righteous cry out, and the LORD hears them;
 he delivers them from all their troubles.
The LORD is close to the brokenhearted
 and saves those who are crushed in spirit.

         —Psalm 34:17–18

Trust in him at all times, O people;
 pour out your hearts to him,
  for God is our refuge.

         —Psalm 62:8

In my anguish I cried to the LORD,
 and he answered by setting me free.

         —Psalm 118:5

When I called, you answered me;
 you made me bold and stouthearted.

         —Psalm 138:3

And will not God bring about justice for his chosen ones, who cry out to him day and night?

         —Luke 18:7

Part 2

ILLUMINATION

CHAPTER 6

ℐ'M SORRY, DADDY

Childlike Remorse

In an alabaster palace, a hall of gilded mirrors
I caught sight of my own reflection:
Filthy rags,
Face smeared with soot,
Hair nested with grease and lice
Abhorrence
Feet bruised, bleeding, encrusted with sludge.

Quaking with horror,
I hid my eyes and turned to run.
Aimlessly, racing through shadows,
I collapsed with nowhere to go;
Lost, terrified
Alone
Weeping uncontrollably through the night.

Just as dawn slipped in,
Gentle Arms
Caressed, calmed, carried me

Back to the mirror,
Urging me to look again.
Amazement.
A princess in radiant white stared back at me,
Looking vaguely like the King Himself.
                    —JEANNE GOWEN DENNIS
                    "REDEMPTION"

PRINCE OR PRINCESS IN DISGUISE

"Mary, come in and try on your flower-girl dress," her mother called out the window as we all waited in the bedroom.

My five-year-old niece ran inside to where her mother and aunts were waiting. Shyly, she shed her play clothes and donned her flower-girl dress for the first time. As Aunt Diana led Mary to the full-length mirror, I caught a whiff of sweat, dirt, and fresh air. A grin lit up Mary's face when she saw herself, and for the next fifteen minutes, she turned and posed, admiring her reflection in the lacy white gown.

I could only imagine what delightful images were running through her mind. *I look like a bride.* She spun around, twisting her torso to watch the long satin skirt billow out. *I'm Cinderella at the ball.* She didn't seem to notice her smudged face or the messy hair falling bramblelike to her shoulders. *I'm beautiful!* Blinded by the white purity of the dress, the child was unaware of her ragged appearance.

Mary didn't know it, but in a small way she was seeing herself as God sees us, as His little princesses and princes in disguise. Are you ready to don your royal robes, or, like my niece, are you encrusted with grime from playing out in the wildwood? Perhaps you feel like a Cinderella waiting for the fairy godmother who never comes. You long to see the King, yet when you look at yourself, you know that you can never be clean enough or good enough to enter His royal presence.

Perhaps you are a man who feels like the fairy tale prince trapped in a frog's body. An evil spell has been cast on you, and you cannot escape until a kind princess takes pity on you and kisses your muddy lips. Then you find out that, contrary to popular belief, the fairy tale was wrong. No princess has the power to release you from your frog skin. Only the King Himself has the power to free you and transform you into the prince you were born to be. Only He can make you clean and worthy to wear the royal robes of His kingdom, and He lovingly waits to do just that.

The King sees us for what we can become. But first, we must see ourselves as we really are.

AWAKENING TO SIN

Waiting on the couch in the living room of my best friend's home, I eyed the candy dish on the coffee table. It was filled with hard candies, and I *really* wanted one. At seven, I was too shy to initiate a conversation with adults, so even if one of her parents had been in the room, I would have been too nervous to ask permission to eat a piece. I kept hoping someone would come in and say, "Have some candy," but no one did. My heart was fighting a battle, and I was losing it fast.

As I pondered my options, I thought that perhaps I could pop a piece in my mouth and eat it before anyone returned. I tried to convince myself that candy sitting on the coffee table was placed there for guests to help themselves. I saw myself as a guest, but I was also a child, and that usually disqualified me from "guest" status. Several times I reached a hand toward the dish and pulled it back. Finally, I grabbed a piece and stuck it in my mouth. My conscience pricked me as I tried to get it down, and then my friend walked in and sat beside me. She noticed.

"Did you take some candy?" she asked incredulously.

"I thought it would be okay, since it was sitting out," I said half-truthfully. "Will I get in trouble?"

"We're not allowed to take candy unless we ask first. That's my dad's candy."

Mortified, I begged her not to tell on me. The guilt of my deed haunted me for weeks. It was the first time that I had willingly and knowingly sinned.

Do you remember the first time you came face-to-face with the fact that you are a sinner? With my perfectionist tendencies, it devastated me. I had failed the test. I discovered that I was not the perfect little angel I had thought myself to be.

To feel so much guilt over eating a piece of candy may seem ridiculous to some, but God gave us the gift of conscience as a deterrent to sin. One little sin, one small compromise usually leads to others. Eventually, as we learn to rationalize and excuse our failures, we find ourselves caught up in bigger and uglier thoughts, words, and actions. Then one day God in His grace shows us a clear vision of ourselves, and we come to our senses. The realization that because of our choices, our loving Savior suffered the excruciating pain of torture and crucifixion is heartrending, even if we never intended to hurt Him or anyone else. Even if the worst sin we committed was to steal a piece of candy.

Unintentional Sin

Sometimes we sin against others or against God without meaning to do harm, and yet the results of our unwise choices do irreparable harm. Author Sheila Seifert wrote to me recalling a Thanksgiving when she was seven or eight that made a lifelong impression on her:

> Extended family and friends gathered at my parents' home every year for Thanksgiving. One year, though, is especially vivid in my mind. I was in the kitchen helping my mother get all the fixings together. My long brown hair was held back by a scarf, and I felt so grown up. My mother put the sliced turkey on a large ceramic platter. While she carried a steaming bowl of stuffing into the next room, I eyed that platter. It looked heavy, but I knew I could carry it. To have the honor of carrying my mother's favorite dish would be the crowning glory of my day. I lifted it with both hands but had barely stepped back from the cupboard when the weight of the loaded dish overcame my strength. The platter crashed to the floor and splintered into a million pieces.

My mother re-entered the kitchen, and I saw the disappointment in her eyes, even as her words told me that everything would be okay. I knew how important the platter was to my mother and the turkey to my family. My thoughtless action had hurt everyone around me. Sobs rose from deep inside, the kind that hurt even as they are coming to the surface. I had broken something that I could never replace. I had messed up in a way that could not be fixed.

In the same way, sin breaks many "platters," and something priceless is lost. When we realize this, we can do nothing but grieve. From within ourselves, there are no words, no consolation, that will fix what is broken.

King David wrote, "Who can discern his errors? Acquit me of hidden faults. Also keep back Your servant from presumptuous sins; let them not rule over me" (Ps. 19:12–13 NASB).

Though sometimes sin is not the result of a conscious decision, we often bring hurt to others by our careless actions or omissions. When temptation does occur, however, our tendency is to beckon to its call like children to the legendary Pied Piper.

THE LURE OF SIN

I was on the phone talking with my sister Christine in Florida. Suddenly, she called out, "Where are the twins? Teddy, Mary, where are your brothers?"

I could hear the children scurrying around as my sister frantically searched the house, still holding the portable phone.

"Who left the door unlocked?" she asked the children. Then she said to me, "The twins are out. I've gotta go!" Click.

This scenario repeated itself day after day from the time the twins learned how to turn a doorknob until they were three years old. Every time they could find an unlocked door, they ran outside, straight for the street in front of the house. It didn't matter to them that they would be punished. The thrill of racing outside and outwitting their mother and older siblings was apparently worth the risk. But after their punishment, they always reached out for their mom to hold and comfort them. They knew their relationship with her had been harmed, and they wanted the assurance that she still loved them, no matter how disobedient they had been.

During that time, my sister dealt with continual stress and fear that one or both of her babies would be hit by a car the second she turned her back. As bad as her stress was, the consequences of the twins' actions could have been much worse, even deadly.

That's the way sin is. It looks desirable, even thrilling. When we answer its alluring call, it begins the conditioning process. It offers pleasures that we can't seem to live without. We compromise more and more as it reels us in closer and closer, gradually blinding us and numbing our senses. Then it sinks its talons deep into our souls, forcing us to become its slaves.

THE SHOCK OF REALITY

Six-year-old Michael hid in the corner of the family room behind the open storage closet door. He pulled the book of matches from his pocket and struck one. The colors in the dancing flame fascinated him. When he felt the heat grow intense on his fingers, he blew out the match. He checked to see if anyone was coming. He'd be in big trouble if he were caught. He lit another match and touched it to the remains of the first match. The cardboard shriveled in smoke and flame.

Just above his head the birdcage cover hung on the door handle. Michael looked at it and wondered how it would burn. He would only singe the edge, that's all. Lighting another match, he lifted it to touch the flowing fabric. It caught fire immediately. Before he realized what was happening, the fire jumped to the row of stored clothes covered by dry cleaning plastic. Flames shot out above his head and spread throughout the closet. A few minutes later, he and the rest of the family shivered outside in the late winter cold as billows of black smoke spewed from the house.

Can you imagine how my little brother felt watching that scene? How devastating it was for him when the fire marshal questioned him later and he had to admit what he had done? Michael had experimented with matches before, knowing that it was not allowed, and nothing bad had come of it. But this time the consequences were far worse than he could have imagined. For three months, eight of us lived in two rooms of a motel while the house was being repaired. My parents didn't have enough insurance to cover the damage and had to refinance the house. Three of us lost everything we owned except the clothes on our backs, and all of us lost things that were precious to us—baby books, photos, drawings, awards, loved toys. Our youngest sister had just celebrated her birthday. All of her new and old toys went up in smoke, and if I had not stopped her from trying to run upstairs to find her shoes, she would certainly have lost her life as well.

Michael understands that God is gracious and forgives, but even forty years later, he grieves that his "one stupid act" hurt Mom and Dad and the rest of the family so much.

"If only I had grabbed the birdcage cover and stomped out the first flames . . ." he says. "Something like that can't help but leave a deep mark inside. I know life goes on, but it's still very painful for me. I remember every detail, how I sat there and couldn't get over the fact that everything I had, all the toys I had played with, were gone. Completely destroyed."

Our slavery to sin brings consequences that we cannot escape, and we long for forgiveness. We need someone to rescue us from our slavery and carry us to our Father's palace, someone with a love so great that it will eclipse all evil and finally bring us peace. That rescue, that love is what the next chapter will discuss.

> Tremble, my soul, and mourn for grief,
>   That such a foe should seize thy breast;
> Fly to thy Lord for quick relief;
>   Oh may he slay this treach'rous guest!
> Then to thy throne, victorious King,
>   Then to thy throne our shouts shall rise!
> Thine everlasting arm we sing;
>   For sin, the monster, bleeds and dies.
> —ISAAC WATTS

Child's Play

1. Is there anything you did today that you wish you hadn't done? Draw a picture, write, or act out a scene showing what you would do differently in the same situation if you were living only to please God.

2. God can and will help you overcome sin, bad habits, and anything else that is destroying your peace. Repeatedly say, "In God's strength I have conquered [name the problem]." Believe it and act accordingly.

3. Watch some television commercials and note what advertisers do to convince viewers to buy their products. The devil is slicker than the most skilled advertiser, the master of bait and switch. He'll lure you in with something that looks wonderful and then he'll destroy you. Pray for discernment to recognize temptation. When it comes, run from it with all your might. Don't consider giving in for an instant. Don't look. Don't smell. Don't listen. Don't taste. Don't touch. Run to God!

4. C. S. Lewis wrote, "We are half-hearted creatures, fooling about with drink and sex and ambition when infinite joy is offered us, like an ignorant child who wants to go on making mud pies in a slum because he cannot imagine what is meant by the offer of a holiday at the sea."[1]

   Write a list of the activities that bring you pleasure in life. Circle any that you can compare to the holiday at sea and cross out those that are more like making mud pies in the slum. Pray over your list and ask God to help you trade the slums for the seashore.

5. Have you experienced God's discipline for something you have done wrong? Remember that He is your Father, and He disciplines those He loves (Prov. 3:11–12). Reach out your arms to the sky for your Abba. Imagine Him taking you in His arms to comfort you.

6. Are you seeing too much of evil? Review your activities and make a list of them. Also list your friends and acquaintances. Which

things and people are beneficial for you spiritually, and which ones drag you down? Pray about any changes God might want you to make.

7. Read and meditate on Psalm 101.

DADDY SAYS SO

About Sin

> When I kept silent,
>   my bones wasted away
>   through my groaning all day long.
> For day and night
>   your hand was heavy upon me;
> my strength was sapped
>   as in the heat of summer.
>
> —Psalm 32:3–4

This righteousness from God comes through faith in Jesus Christ to all who believe. There is no difference, for all have sinned and fall short of the glory of God, and are justified freely by his grace through the redemption that came by Christ Jesus.

—Romans 3:22–24

How can we who died to sin still live in it? Or are you unaware that all of us who were baptized into Christ Jesus were baptized into His death? Therefore we were buried with Him by baptism into death, in order that, just as Christ was raised from the dead by the glory of the Father, so we too may walk in a new way of life.

—Romans 6:2–4 HCSB

Don't you know that when you offer yourselves to someone to obey him as slaves, you are slaves to the one whom you obey—whether you are slaves to sin, which leads to death, or to obedience, which leads to righteousness?

—Romans 6:16

A man reaps what he sows. The one who sows to please his sinful nature, from that nature will reap destruction; the one who sows to please the Spirit, from the Spirit will reap eternal life.

—Galatians 6:7–8

If we claim to be without sin, we deceive ourselves and the truth is not in us. . . . If we claim we have not sinned, we make him out to be a liar and his word has no place in our lives.

—1 John 1:8, 10

About Temptation

So, if you think you are standing firm, be careful that you don't fall! No temptation has seized you except what is common to man. And God is faithful; he will not let you be tempted beyond what you can bear. But when you are tempted, he will also provide a way out so that you can stand up under it.

—1 Corinthians 10:12–13

But each one is tempted when he is drawn away by his own desires and enticed. Then, when desire has conceived, it gives birth to sin; and sin, when it is full-grown, brings forth death. Do not be deceived, my beloved brethren.

—James 1:14–16 NKJV

Submit yourselves, then, to God. Resist the devil, and he will flee from you.

—James 4:7

About God's Discipline

> My son, do not despise the LORD'S discipline
> and do not resent his rebuke,
> because the LORD disciplines those he loves,
> as a father the son he delights in.
>
> —Proverbs 3:11–12

If you are not disciplined (and everyone undergoes discipline), then you are illegitimate children and not true sons. Moreover, we have all had human fathers who disciplined us and we respected them for it. How much more should we submit to the Father of our spirits and live! Our fathers disciplined us for a little while as they thought best; but God disciplines us for our good, that we may share in his holiness. No discipline seems pleasant at the time, but painful. Later on, however, it produces a harvest of righteousness and peace for those who have been trained by it.

—Hebrews 12:8–11

CHAPTER 7

*M*Y DADDY LOVES ME

Childlike Need for Unconditional Love

> *There is a place of quiet rest*
> *Near to the heart of God.*
> *A place where sin cannot molest,*
> *Near to the heart of God.*
>
> *There is a place of comfort sweet*
> *Near to the heart of God,*
> *A place where we our Savior meet,*
> *Near to the heart of God.*
>
> *There is a place of full release*
> *Near to the heart of God,*
> *A place where all is joy and peace,*
> *Near to the heart of God.*
> —CLELAND B. MCAFEE
> "NEAR TO THE HEART OF GOD"

SIN'S HIGH COST

In Patricia St. John's children's novel *Treasures of the Snow*, a boy who is teasing a younger child accidentally causes the younger boy to become paralyzed. As a result, the older boy loses his friends and the respect of everyone in the small community.

When my brother set the house on fire, his losses were not only material. His bad decision at age six has affected every aspect of his life.

"When I think about it, sometimes there's a very deep sadness that overcomes me," Michael says. "It was a lonely place to be. The scorn of my cousins and the kids at school marked me, and I was ostracized from then on."

Yet we, his siblings, understood. We forgave him because we loved him and because we all had made mistakes too. We also knew that he was only a little child who didn't understand the seriousness of his actions until it was too late. Though we grieved for our losses, we also empathized with his pain.

"One good thing that came out of it," he says, "is that I have tried to make it up to Mom and Dad by being a worthy son. As far as I'm concerned, whatever Mom and Dad want, they get. As a teen, I would work beside them. Even when I was feeling rebellious and didn't want to do it, I'd think back to [the fire] and tell myself, 'I have to do this.' I tried to be there for them as much as I could be. In that time it also allowed me to have a relationship with Mom and Dad that the others didn't have. A lot of things grew from that stupid thing I did, but it still bothers me."

REPAIRING THE DAMAGE

Like Mike, we all have trouble accepting forgiveness when we have done something awful, especially when we know we have caused pain to others. At times like that, even God's forgiveness may not feel like enough, seeming nebulous—out in space somewhere—even though we know intellectually and spiritually that it's real. Out of remorse, we may try to make up for our wrongdoings or feel that we deserve to carry the guilt of our sins for the rest of our lives. But we can do neither. Neither can we undo the damage that has already been done.

As young and innocent as Mike was, his choice to play with matches affected the whole family. Likewise, our disobedience to God takes a toll on us and everyone around us. Although God forgives us when we ask (1 John 1:9), we still often have to suffer the results of our bad choices. Sin kills. Sin destroys. Sin separates us from God. But even after sin and its consequences, we can find hope and unconditional love.

Mark Tabb, author of *Out of the Whirlwind*, points out that even when God allows nature to destroy by fire, flood, hurricane, or drought, the canvas of nature is never wiped totally clean and left that way. God always renews it with beauty. Likewise, God never leaves repentant sinners in their ruined state. He regenerates us from the devastation that sin wreaks in our lives. He forgives and restores. Through His unfailing love, God always makes a way for beauty, peace, and joy to return to our lives when we yield ourselves to Him.

"But what if I've done something unforgivable?" you might ask, "like murder, abortion, rape, adultery, premarital sex, or divorce? What if I knew better and still betrayed my Lord?"

IMPOSSIBLY DIRTY?

Have you ever heard someone say, "God may forgive *you,* but He could never forgive *me*"? Have you said it yourself? Faced with God's holiness and our own wickedness, we may fear that we are too dirty for even God to clean. After going through a season of sinfulness and then coming to our senses, we can see ourselves clearly—as hopelessly evil, which we are in comparison to God's holiness. We may be tempted to think that God couldn't possibly forgive us and wouldn't even want to.

If you feel unforgivable, don't give in to feelings of despair. No matter what you have done or failed to do, no matter how evil you are, Jesus died to pay for your sins. Then He rose from the dead to bring you new life. He wants you to come to Him like a repentant child. When you do, you will find your heavenly Father running to you with open arms while the angels in heaven rejoice (Luke 15:10, 20).

What if you can't relate to all this talk about sinfulness? What if you've never done anything terrible in your whole life?

ALREADY A DEBUTANTE?

If you're one of those blessed people who has managed to steer clear of the sins we view as "really bad," then thank God. And be on your guard. In some ways, you could be in more danger than those who have committed serious sins and repented. "Be self-controlled and alert," the Bible warns. "Your enemy the devil prowls around like a roaring lion looking for someone to devour" (1 Peter 5:8).

Complacency, pride, and overconfidence open the door to temptation. Not discounting the evil of more grievous sins, it is important to remember that in light of God's perfection and holiness, even our tiniest sin is blacker than an unlit coalmine. Examine yourself daily. Have you gossiped about someone or used the Lord's name without giving Him due reverence and respect? Have you viewed (and by default condoned) movies or programs that portray sinful behavior and blasphemy as acceptable? Have you helped yourself to office supplies at work without paying for them? Have you passed up the opportunity to help someone because you were too busy?

Congratulating ourselves on having committed no great sins can be a sin too—the sin of pride. Jesus told a parable about two men who went to the temple to pray. One, a tax collector, acknowledged that he was a terrible sinner; the other, a Pharisee, listed all his good deeds and thanked God that he was not a sinner like other men. The repentant man connected with God; the other man left as sinful as when he came (Luke 18:10–14).

The truth is that our sins, no matter how small or few, deserve the punishment of hell (Matt. 5:21–22, 27–29; Rom. 6:23; James 2:10). Yet God loves us so much that He doesn't want us to live an eternity without Him.

If we confess our sins, he is faithful and just and will forgive us our sins and purify us from all unrighteousness. If we claim we have not sinned, we make him out to be a liar and his word has no place in our lives. (1 John 1:9–10)

Childlike intimacy with God cannot happen until we are completely honest about ourselves and our sinfulness. We all have a desperate need for the unconditional love He offers through forgiveness and the freedom, joy, and peace that it brings.

RESTORING THE BOND

When Carmen's husband left her for another woman, she wondered how her sons would deal with the resulting divorce and the family's severely reduced finances. Six-year-old Justin, who was always a handful, acted out a little, showing his disappointment and anger. Carmen was relieved to see that eight-year-old Nick seemed to be doing okay, but then he had seldom been a problem.

One day, she entered the grocery store with a strict list. She knew she had only twenty dollars for food, and she had figured her groceries to the last penny. When she was ready to check out, she looked for the money in her wallet, but it was gone. She had to leave all the food behind.

How are we going to eat this week? she wondered. *Who could have taken the money?*

At home, she confronted Justin and asked him if he had borrowed the twenty dollars from her purse. "Did you take it to buy candy? Did you borrow it and lose it somewhere?" she asked.

Justin denied taking the money, and since he usually told the truth, Carmen believed him. But she couldn't imagine Nick doing it. He never did anything like that. Still, the money was gone and she needed to find it, so she decided to ask him about it.

"Nick, did you take the twenty dollars I had for food?"

Nick answered simply. "Yes, I did."

"What did you do with it?"

"I walked out onto a bridge and gave it to a boy."

Carmen was really confused. "You mean you gave money to a perfect stranger? Why?"

Nick's face grew angry. "Because I knew you needed it and I wanted to hurt you."

Carmen felt a new kind of pain as she realized what her son was thinking. "Nick, are you trying to hurt me because you're blaming me for the divorce?"

"Yes." Nick broke down and Carmen held him close as they cried together. It was a cleansing moment, a time of shared grief and forgiveness. Nick and his mom were reconciled, and the subject was never mentioned again.

Carmen says, "I believe that moment with the twenty dollars was pivotal to his development. That little boy is now almost twenty-four. . . . He is honest, trustworthy, and such a fine young man."

The unconditional love Carmen demonstrated to her son helped him through a heartrending time in his life and reassured him of his place in her heart. As we grow in our understanding of the love that washes us clean, we too are overwhelmed with the sense of how precious we are.

Washed in Love

Kathy's tummy rumbled and her stomach hurt. A first grader, she was almost ready to leave for school, but something didn't feel right. She headed for the bathroom but didn't make it in time, because both bathrooms were filled with other kids getting ready for school. Not wanting to tell anyone about her problem, she tried to take care of herself, but the odor gave her secret away.

Mom took the other kids to school while Dad led Kathy upstairs for a bath.

Recalling the incident my sister says, "As Dad was cleaning up that awful mess and giving me a bath, I noticed that he was being so gentle! I remember looking up at him and thinking, *He must really love me to do this for me.*"

Jesus demonstrated the same tender love to His disciples the night before He died. The Passover Feast had been prepared, and the apostles were assembled in the Upper Room with Him. Everything was ready, except that no one had washed their feet, a task usually reserved for a servant. Dirt from the roads of Jerusalem felt grimy inside their sandals. To everyone's amazement, Jesus got up, took off his outer clothing, filled a basin, and began washing the feet of each apostle in turn (John 13:1–5).

On that night, God in human form lowered Himself to serve not only His faithful followers, but also Judas, the friend and disciple who was about to betray Him. And what a mess Jesus must have had to clean! Traveling the dusty roads of ancient Jerusalem would have made sandaled feet disgustingly dirty. As Jesus progressed from one disciple to the next, more and more dirt undoubtedly clouded the basin. When He was finished, the water must have been thick with grime, a fitting symbol of the sin, the disgusting filth, He would die the next day to cleanse.

While the sins of the whole world weighed heavily on Jesus, the pain and anguish must have been excruciating beyond imagination. Yet He chose to carry that burden. He was the only one who could. It was necessary to save His people from the evil power of sin—to both allow and prepare them to live forever with Him.

DRESSED IN PUREST WHITE

Jesus says to all of us, "Come to me, all you who are weary and burdened, and I will give you rest" (Matt. 11:28).

Our guilt and our sin are more than we can bear. That's why God Himself wants to—and has to—carry it. His love for us is stronger than any evil we have done. When we come to Him as little children, sorry for our sinfulness, He removes our sullied play clothes, washes us inside and out, and covers us with raiment of purest white—made from the fabric of His perfection. Then we can enter God's presence clean and new, like the princes and princesses we were born to be.

The Father hears Him pray,
His dear Anointed One;
He cannot turn away
The presence of His Son;
His Spirit answers to the blood,
And tells me, I am born of God.

My God is reconciled,
His pardoning voice I hear;
He owns me for His child,
I can no longer fear;
With confidence I now draw nigh,
And Father, Abba Father, cry!

—CHARLES WESLEY
"BEHOLD THE MAN!"

CHILD'S PLAY

1. When you realize that you have done something wrong, ask God's forgiveness right away. Name the sin. Confront it, and then give it to Jesus. He's already taken your punishment. Then believe you are forgiven, because that's His promise. Read 1 John 1.

2. If you have done something for which you can make restitution—in other words, pay for or help to remedy the hurt you have caused others—then do it now. Remember God's love for you, and let Him love others through you.

3. If you're holding on to guilt for sins you've already confessed, then let it go right now. Imagine that your guilt is a heavy pack on your back. Take it off and hand it to Jesus. He already took your burdens at the cross. Remember that God separates our sins from us "as far as the east is from the west" (Ps. 103:12).

4. Read Luke 15. Meditate on God's amazing love, compassion, redemption, and forgiveness.

5. Make yourself a dandelion crown. Wear it as you praise your Father, the King, for making you heavenly royalty in disguise. Or

find a stick and pretend it is a sword. Imagine your King knighting you with that sword.

6. Remember what your life without Jesus was like, and thank God for saving you. Paint a picture or write a poem or song about what Jesus' sacrifice means to you.

7. Lie on your back outside. Close your eyes and relish the warmth of sunshine and the freshness of the breeze. Breathe deeply of the fresh air. Delight in the sounds and scents of life around you and listen for God's whisper that says, "I love you."

DADDY SAYS SO

About Confession and Remorse

> Look upon my affliction and my distress
> and take away all my sins.
>
> —Psalm 25:18

> Blessed is the man
>   whose sin the LORD does not count against him
>   and in whose spirit is no deceit.
> When I kept silent,
>   my bones wasted away
>   through my groaning all day long.
> For day and night
>   your hand was heavy upon me;
> my strength was sapped
>   as in the heat of summer.
> Then I acknowledged my sin to you
>   and did not cover up my iniquity.
> I said, "I will confess
>   my transgressions to the LORD"—

and you forgave
   the guilt of my sin.

                              —Psalm 32:2–5

If we confess our sins, he is faithful and just and will forgive us our
sins and purify us from all unrighteousness.

                              —1 John 1:9

About God's Forgiveness

Surely he took up our infirmities
   and carried our sorrows,
yet we considered him stricken by God,
   smitten by him, and afflicted.
But he was pierced for our transgressions,
   he was crushed for our iniquities;
the punishment that brought us peace was upon him,
   and by his wounds we are healed.
We all, like sheep, have gone astray,
   each of us has turned to his own way;
and the LORD has laid on him
   the iniquity of us all.

                              —Isaiah 53:4–6

Who is a God like you,
   who pardons sin and forgives the transgression
   of the remnant of his inheritance?
You do not stay angry forever
   but delight to show mercy.

                              —Micah 7:18

For God so loved the world that he gave his one and only Son, that
whoever believes in him shall not perish but have eternal life. For
God did not send his Son into the world to condemn the world,
but to save the world through him. Whoever believes in him is not

condemned, but whoever does not believe stands condemned already because he has not believed in the name of God's one and only Son.

—John 3:16–18

. . . and I lay down my life for the sheep.

—John 10:15

For one will hardly die for a righteous man; though perhaps for the good man someone would dare even to die. But God demonstrates His own love toward us, in that while we were yet sinners, Christ died for us.

—Romans 5:7–8 NASB

$\mathcal{S}$AVE ME, DADDY!

Childlike Need for a Rescuer

> We were crowded in the cabin,
> Not a soul would dare to sleep,—
> It was midnight on the water,
> And a storm was on the deep.
>
> 'Tis a fearful thing in winter
> To be shattered by the blast,
> And to hear the rattling trumpet
> Thunder, "Cut away the mast!"
>
> So we shuddered there in silence,—
> For the stoutest held his breath,
> While the hungry sea was roaring
> And the breakers talked with death.
>
> As thus we sat in darkness,
> Each one busy with his prayers,
> "We are lost!" the captain shouted,
> As he staggered down the stairs.

But his little daughter whispered,
As she took his icy hand,
"Isn't God upon the ocean,
Just the same as on the land?"

Then we kissed the little maiden,
And we spake in better cheer,
And we anchored safe in harbor
When the morn was shining clear.

—JAMES THOMAS FIELDS
"BALLAD OF THE TEMPEST"

HE ANSWERS WHEN WE CALL

In the wee hours of morning, I bundled up under a blanket in the car to go skiing. "Do you think the roads will be clear?" I asked Steve. A Colorado native, he possessed superior winter driving skills, but snowy mountain roads petrified me.

"We'll be fine," he said. I could tell that he hoped for a blizzard and fresh powder.

He got his wish. The further into the mountains we drove, the worse the visibility and the roads became. As we crested a steep hill, we saw with horror that a disabled car was blocking our lane. There was no escape—no shoulder and no break in the line of cars in the left lane. Steve pumped his brakes and our car went into a spin. Then we headed backward downhill at increasing speed—straight for the stopped car. A wall of rock bordered the road on one side and a steep precipice on the other. I knew there was no way we could escape a collision alive.

It had only been a few months since I had turned my life over to Jesus. Steve didn't believe as I did, and I had never prayed aloud in front of him. But as death approached, I was desperate. "Jesus, help us!" I cried aloud.

Steve told me later that at that moment he "heard" a voice telling him to take his foot off the brake. He did, and we both felt the car being lifted and turned around. When we were facing forward again, our car was within a few feet of the disabled car and still moving fast. Suddenly there was a space in the left lane, and with literally seconds to spare, Steve swerved around the other car as if on a cushion of air. Mouths gaping, we wondered if those behind us realized that they had just witnessed a miracle. That day, we experienced firsthand that God answers when we call on Jesus' name.

DADDY, SAVE ME!

Some rescues are large like that day on the mountain, and some are small.

Little fingers waved at the end of outstretched arms. "Daddy, save me!" A little girl stood at the top of a brick wall, hovering over the sidewalk, but she didn't need help. She had climbed up there herself— over and over again. It was a game she played, assuring herself that her knight in shining armor, her daddy, would race to her rescue whenever she beckoned.

Just like that little girl's confidence in her daddy, our hope in Jesus Christ is a certainty, not a wish. Sometimes He races immediately to our rescue, and other times, for reasons we may not understand, He makes us wait.

At the top of a narrow staircase, all seven of us—Mom, Dad, and the five kids—stopped in front of an apartment door. We were all excited to visit our uncle and aunt's new apartment. At Mom's knock, the door opened and we were ushered inside. I was the last one in, and as the door was closing, I noticed three-year-old Kathy standing on the threshold. She backed up as the door closed in her face. I tried to tell the adults that she was outside, but they were all talking excitedly. I pulled on Mom's arm. "Mommy, Ka—." Then I tried Dad, but no one heard me. I thought about opening the door myself, but at age five I was afraid to take that bold step without permission. Finally, my aunt asked, "Where's Kathy?"

Finally! I thought.

When the door was opened, we saw Kathy sitting patiently on the steps, simply waiting for help.

We often have to wait for God to come to our rescue. When the waiting feels interminable, we can only trust.

Steve was out of town and four-year-old Christine was ill. Hour after hour, I gave her medicine, liquids, and chicken soup. She couldn't sleep, and as was usually the case when she was ill, her temperature was extremely high, hovering around 104 or 105 degrees. I wasn't sure what to do, and our doctor discouraged calls in the middle of the night.

As I watched Christine's flushed face, I needed my husband's help and advice, but he was thousands of miles away. I wished I had a nearby relative or friend I could call on, but I could think of no one who would want to come to my rescue in the middle of the night.

Finally, I noticed Christine growing tired. *Good*, I thought. *Maybe we can both get some sleep.* Then I realized she was lethargic. When she spoke, her words made no sense. Suddenly she pointed to the ceiling and giggled uncontrollably. Alarmed, I asked her why she was laughing.

"The angels are funny. They're having a race." She giggled again. "Look!"

At that moment, I was sure my child was dying. I begged God to save her and tell me what to do to get the fever down. If I cooled her too quickly, I knew she would shiver and the fever would rise. Then I remembered a technique a nurse had shown me when Christine had a high fever as an infant. I swooped her up in my arms and carried her into the bathroom. Then I wrapped cool, wet cloths around her extremities, and as the cloths warmed from the fever, I replaced them with cooler and cooler ones. All the while, I prayed silently and tried to keep Christine involved in conversation.

Finally, after what seemed like days to me, her fever subsided, and she was herself again. As I tucked her back into bed and she fell into a peaceful sleep, I fell trembling, crying, and exhausted to my knees. Though it seemed to take forever, God came to my rescue in time. No matter what our circumstances, we can take comfort that He is in control.

He Reigns from Heaven

One summer afternoon in Denver, my friend Risa and I sat in a park watching our daughters skate. Christine, Jennifer, and Laura relished the freedom of having wheels under their feet and plenty of room to race the wind. As I followed their progress across the park, I noticed an indigo-gray cloud on the northern horizon. I tapped Risa's shoulder.

"Look at that. It's still miles away, but it looks ominous."

"Let's have the girls skate in the direction of the parking lot, just in case," she suggested.

Before we had a chance to explain our plan to the children, the cloud doubled in size and progressed toward us at an alarming rate. There wasn't time to remove skates. We pulled our skating girls along as we raced for the parking lot.

Suddenly, the wind started pushing as we pulled. Leaves, trash, and our hair blew around our faces, making it difficult to see. Just as we reached the opposite side of the park, rain and hail began to pelt us. We partly dragged and partly carried the girls up a steep flight of cement steps leading to the parking lot. Then we scrambled to get the car unlocked and jam our picnic supplies and ourselves inside.

No shelter was available to shield the car from the now golf ball–size hail, so we started for home. I knew it was only a matter of seconds before the windows would shatter in around us.

"I need support," I yelled to the others.

"What?"

"Pray!"

They assured me that they were all praying. But I knew it wasn't enough. I recalled my Bible reading from that morning. In preparing to go into battle with a huge army, King Jehoshaphat placed musicians in front of his troops. They praised God with loud, joyous music as they marched, because they knew that God would fight their battle (2 Chron. 20:1–24).

"I need more support," I shouted again through the deafening cracks and crashes.

"Like what?" my companions responded, understandably wondering how they could possibly help me get us home safely.

"Sing. . . . Sing praises to the Lord."

The only song we could think of was "Awesome God." We did our best to drown out the storm's invective with our voices. Our singing was sugared with laughter at the pun where the song mentions God reigning from heaven. So we sang, laughed, and skidded all the way home. Surprisingly, the windows held firm, but I was concerned about how Steve would feel about the inevitable damage to the rest of our new car.

We found out later that the storm caused about $626 million in damage to homes and vehicles across the Denver area. Many cars caught in the storm were totaled by insurance companies. Others had shattered windows and bore deep pockmarked scars from their battle with the elements. But the car in which we sang praises to God had no damage at all—not one dent.

The Bible indicates that God inhabits the praises of His people (Ps. 22:3 KJV), and Jesus said that He is present where two or more are gathered in His name (Matt. 18:20). God was with us as we praised Him through that storm, and His presence protected both us and the car. That's the only explanation we have.

Christine and I shared this story with Rich Mullins, the popular Christian singer who composed the song "Awesome God." We told him how God used a summer outing, a record-breaking hailstorm, and his song to demonstrate to us just how awesome our God really is. God rescued us, but sadly for the thousands of people who were blessed by Rich's ministry, God didn't prevent the car accident that killed Rich Mullins in 1997.

If God is our Rescuer, then why doesn't He rescue all of us all of the time? There is no satisfactory answer to that question—at least not in this life. In a world tainted by sin, trouble and pain are facts of life. God hears and answers our prayers, just not always in our timing or in our way. We can trust God to protect us and rescue us when we call on Him. However, when the unthinkable happens, we need to crawl on our heavenly Daddy's lap and ask Him to hold us.

If on a quiet sea,
Toward heaven we calmly sail,
With grateful hearts, O God, to thee,
We'll own the favoring gale.

But should the surges rise,
And rest delay to come,
Blest be the tempest, kind the storm,
Which drives us nearer home.

Soon shall our doubts and fears
All yield to thy control;
Thy tender mercies shall illume
The mid-night of the soul.

Teach us, in every state,
To make thy will our own;
And when the joys of sense depart,
To live by faith alone.

—AUGUSTUS TOPLADY
"IF ON A QUIET SEA"

CHILD'S PLAY

1. To help you get ready for potential fears in the future, remember a few times in the past when you were afraid. Sing praises to God because He brought you through those times. If you can't sing, praise Him in your heart.
2. Memorize Scripture verses (found at the end of this chapter) that reassure you of God's care for you. When you need them, God will bring them to your mind.
3. Read Psalms 9 and 116 and meditate on them. Notice that praising God goes hand in hand with His protection. Praise Him for His faithfulness.

4. Don't be afraid or ashamed to call on the name of Jesus. Sometimes only He stands between us and disaster. The next time you need His help, ask Him out loud. In fact, talk to Him right now, out loud, and thank Him for allowing you to call on His name, the name that opens heaven's gates for you.

5. When God doesn't come to your rescue, even when you've asked Him to, hold on more tightly to Him than ever. He knows the past, the present, and the future, and He knows what's best for us. We may never know His reasons, but we must trust Him. Hold on to a solid building as a reminder that God is with you. He is your Rock in times of distress, whether you can sense His presence or not.

6. Think about learning to ride a bicycle. At first, the learner is stiff and wobbly on the bike, but as he or she gains confidence, the ride becomes smoother. Experienced riders will lean into the curves in the road. As we travel the path of life and encounter the curves of trouble and pain, our ride will be smoother if we lean into Jesus.

7. Find someone who has suffered a recent loss or crisis. If you don't know anyone personally, then ask at your church or look in the newspaper for names. Pray in the name of Jesus for the people involved. Then write a note of sympathy or encouragement and send it in care of the church or editor. If you can help in a more tangible way, then do that as well.

DADDY SAYS SO

About God's Presence with Us

> Even though I walk
>   through the valley of the shadow of death,
> I will fear no evil,
>   for you are with me;
> your rod and your staff,
>   they comfort me.

—Psalm 23:4

Do not fear, for I am with you;
Do not anxiously look about you, for I am your God.
I will strengthen you, surely I will help you,
Surely I will uphold you with My righteous right hand.

—Isaiah 41:10 NASB

For where two or three have gathered together in My name, I am there in their midst.

—Matthew 18:20 NASB

About Trusting God in Fear or Trouble

I look for your deliverance, O LORD.

—Genesis 49:18

The LORD also will be a refuge for the oppressed,
A refuge in times of trouble.
And those who know Your name will put their trust in You;
For You, LORD, have not forsaken those who seek You.

—Psalm 9:9–10 NKJV

Keep me safe, O God,
    for in you I take refuge.

—Psalm 16:1

Taste and see that the LORD is good;
    blessed is the man who takes refuge in him.

—Psalm 34:8

The salvation of the righteous comes from the LORD;
    he is their stronghold in time of trouble.

—Psalm 37:39

God is our refuge and strength,
    an ever-present help in trouble.

Therefore we will not fear, though the earth give way
 and the mountains fall into the heart of the sea,
though its waters roar and foam
 and the mountains quake with their surging.

         —Psalm 46:1–3

If you make the Most High your dwelling—
 even the LORD, who is my refuge—
then no harm will befall you,
 no disaster will come near your tent.

         —Psalm 91:9–10

"Because he loves me," says the LORD, "I will rescue him;
 I will protect him, for he acknowledges my name.
He will call upon me, and I will answer him;
 I will be with him in trouble,
 I will deliver him and honor him.
With long life will I satisfy him
 and show him my salvation."

         —Psalm 91:14–16

I was pushed back and about to fall,
 but the LORD helped me.
The LORD is my strength and my song;
 he has become my salvation.

         —Psalm 118:13–14

$\mathcal{D}$ADDY, HOLD ME!

Childlike Need for Comfort

Another dream has run aground. It tumbled overboard and drowned.
I feel betrayed. It's hard to pray.
Nothing turned out as I planned. I thought I saw Your guiding hand.
Was I mistaken? My faith is shaken.
I know You're somewhere in the dark, that we're not really far apart,
and You can show the way to go.
For You are higher than the stars. You can see from where You are
my next horizon. I'll keep my eyes on You.

You're the peace in my storm.
I'm a fragile little boat. Won't you send a breeze of hope to fill my sail?
Peace in my storm,
When the howling winds increase, only You can make them cease.
Calm the seas by Your power. Jesus, be my Harbor,
so safe and warm, Peace in my storm.

—JEANNE GOWEN DENNIS
"PEACE IN MY STORM"

DADDY, FIX IT!

"Paste it, Daddy," cries little Zuzu after petals fall from the flower she carried home from school. Her father turns away and hides the stray petals in his pocket. Then he assures her that the flower is as good as new. Confident that her daddy has solved her problem and comforted by his touch, the child lies back to go to sleep.

Everyone who has watched the classic movie *It's a Wonderful Life* is familiar with that sweet scene. It epitomizes the cry of every child who believes that her daddy can fix any damaged treasure, solve any problem, or soothe any hurt. What a shock it can be to find out that our earthly fathers can't fix everything! It's an even greater shock to discover that the omnipotent God who *has* the power to do something about our problems sometimes chooses not to bring us immediate comfort and "fix it."

TREASURE THROUGH PAIN

When my niece Mary was just learning to read, I took her to the doctor for a checkup. Since I lived two thousand miles away, we didn't have much time to spend together. As she waited in the cold, antiseptic-tainted examination room, I held her close, wrapped in my arms and my sweater, and we read a children's magazine together. On the rebus pages, we took turns; I read the words and she "read" the pictures. We laughed at the jokes and riddles. Then I read her a story. Finally, the doctor came in, checked Mary, and pronounced her healthy.

"It's time for shots," the pediatrician announced. Mary's fearful look prompted the doctor to continue. "Don't worry. It won't hurt. You'll only feel a little prick."

The doctor asked me to hold down my niece's arms while a nurse held down her legs. As I watched the long, thick needle approaching Mary's thin leg, I tried to block her view of it. I knew the doctor had lied. That needle was going to hurt—a lot. Stoically, Mary waited, but when the needle entered her flesh, she stiffened and whimpered, tears spilling from her eyes. After administering the shots, the doctor and nurse left, and Mary clung to me, sobbing. I could do nothing to comfort her except hold her in my lap as my tears mingled with hers. The next day, Mary asked me to take her to the doctor whenever she needed shots. She knew that I wouldn't be able to help her avoid the pain, but she also knew that I would walk through it with her.

We are told that God allows pain in our lives because we need it to grow, to change, or perhaps to develop a closer relationship with Him or another person. Just as I tried to do for Mary, God walks through our pain with us. Unlike me, God *can* prevent suffering, but often chooses not to. Intellectually, we can accept that He knows our needs better than we do and that He will use the pain for our good. However, when we are going through it, we can't understand and don't want to hear about how good it might be for us in the long run. Some agony is so severe that no explanation will suffice.

Trust Alone

Before Suzanne Haley's sons and their friends left Colorado on a trip to California, the family gathered and prayed for God's protection over the travelers. However, in the early hours of the next morning, the car skidded on a patch of ice and Suzanne's teenage son, Sean, was killed. Now, several years later, Suzanne can't understand why God allowed her son to die on that dark, icy road. "Even if God came down and told me why He took Sean," she says, "I still wouldn't be satisfied. All I can do is trust that God is God."

Speaker Lee McDowell prayed for years for her brother, her closest sibling, to walk with the Lord. Then she lost him to suicide. That week, McDowell had been memorizing Matthew 21:22: "If you believe, you will receive whatever you ask for in prayer."

She says, "I believed that I would see that prayer answered more than anything I'd ever prayed for in those nineteen years, but God could not answer my prayer after the suicide. I was angry with God. He is sovereign; He could have prevented it and didn't."

McDowell recalls entering an intense spiritual crisis after her brother's death. Since childhood, she had believed what someone told her, that she would die if she ever got angry. For thirty-five years, she had not allowed anger to surface. After her brother's suicide, she was no longer able to deny anger in herself.

"I became honest about anger for the first time in my life. Job (after Jesus) became my best friend in Scripture. . . . He didn't seek to hide his humanity from God. . . . Anger is intense honesty with God, but God is much bigger than anger. He created us with the capacity for anger. . . . It's what we do with it that matters."

A HEAVENLY PERSPECTIVE ON TROUBLE

In recent years, McDowell went through thirty-four months of crisis. First, her husband, Clyde, a godly, vibrant seminary president and former pastor, contracted brain cancer and died at the age of forty-nine after a year-long illness. Sixteen months later her sister died suddenly, and eighteen months after that her mother died, just three weeks after being diagnosed with pancreatic cancer. McDowell says:

> When my closest sibling committed suicide, I had worked through what God's promises really mean and [saw] a much bigger framework for interpreting them than just this slice of history—my life and my culture. When my husband became ill, we had been in ministry together for twenty-four years plus, so we had seen many people, many godly and good people suffer much. . . . And so we understood that when [Scripture] says that God will take care of us or that He will not allow us to experience more trial than we can possibly bear, it doesn't mean that He will not allow us to experience that which is almost worse than we could have imagined, but that He will give us the grace to endure and persevere in the midst of it.
>
> I look at these truths—that God will take care of us, but this horrific [event] occurred—as paradoxical . . . seemingly contradictory, but actually both true, in almost two different realms of reality. There's the material world where physical harm does occur. There's the spiritual realm of reality where nothing can touch us. . . . [Most] of the time we live down here in the material, and the fact is here,

we do get hurt, and yet God is ultimately caring for us in ways that are often not apparent to us at the time. . . . God is good and has purposes that are far bigger than I can ever imagine.[1]

Now, on the other side of her three-year nightmare, McDowell says that she would rather be here than anywhere else. "I have more intimacy with God than ever, and I wouldn't trade it. I wouldn't want to *not* know what I have come to understand of the nature of God through my experience. It's an intimate and personal knowledge of the soul, not the head."[2]

Even when we can't feel His presence, somewhere in the dark night of our troubles, God is there.

SOMEWHERE IN THE DARK

A few years ago, I taught a kindergarten Sunday school class. We were studying about how God always takes care of us, but many of the children in my class had serious problems in their lives. One child lost both his grandfather and his mother within a few weeks. My little, innocent five- and six-year-old students prayed about surgeries, unemployment, financial struggles, divorces, illnesses, and deaths. I was grateful that they didn't ask the obvious question, "Why does God protect some and not others?" because I didn't know how to answer it.

Yet I still believe that God takes care of us, because I believe the Scriptures and have experienced God's loving care in my own life. Down deep I know that God loves those who suffer and grieve and has a good plan for their lives. But that doesn't remove the pain. Author and speaker Sandra Aldrich says that losing a loved one is like an amputation. "[It] will always be an amputation," she says, "but it does not always have to bleed."[3]

The scars we suffer in a world made imperfect through Adam's sin may never go away, although after a time of healing we can look at them as a reminder, not of what we suffered, but of all that God has brought us through. With our finite minds we cannot understand why God allows evil to flourish, why He sometimes intervenes and often does not. We just need to remember and believe—especially when it's difficult—that God is faithful. God *does* take care of us.

FRAGILE BOAT

A few years ago, I faced my own faith crisis when I thought I might lose four members of my family all within a few months. My parents, both in their eighties, were struggling with serious health problems and prearranged their funerals while two of my sisters were battling cancer. Overwhelmed with grief in the darkened room where I usually pray each night, I tried to kneel, but couldn't. I fell into a sitting position and clutched my legs to my chest, sobbing. I needed a daddy's comfort, but my father was two thousand miles away. Without words, leaning my head against the bed, I mentally climbed on my heavenly Daddy's lap. I couldn't pray. All I could say was, "Please, God. Please." Eventually, my sobs subsided, but I still sat there, waiting for the peace that only He can give. I wasn't overwhelmed with peace as I have been at times in the past, but I felt that He had calmed my mind and soul.

Since then, my sisters have shown no more signs of cancer and my parents have experienced improved health. It was a year of uncertainty and pain for our family, but through it, we knew God's peace.

PEACE IN MY STORM

In 2004, I entered a season of hope. My family members were healthy, and best of all, our first grandchild was on the way. But on the evening that I celebrated the completion of the first draft of this book, our daughter went into labor four and a half months early. The next morning, she called and tearfully told me that her baby had been born alive but died within a few minutes. Her grief was understandably intense, but I was not prepared for my own grief.

Watching my daughter and son-in-law go through such excruciating emotional pain and feeling the loss of my grandchild so keenly led me into a three-month battle with depression. Also, several pending book contracts were canceled. My season of hope had turned into a season of loss. While working on the first draft of this manuscript, I had talked about having total trust in God, no matter what He might bring us through. When my first grandchild died, I had to live out what I had written.

God has our welfare in mind. I believe that everything we suffer will be used for our good (Rom. 8:28–29). However, in the midst of pain and uncertainty, it is difficult to appreciate that fact. Sometimes I feel angry that God doesn't change the circumstances. Then I have to face the reality that God is God, and He has the right to do whatever He pleases with His creatures.

During that time, my daughter also struggled and learned to trust God in new ways. A month after their loss, she wrote:

> I have learned things about God that I never would have had I not been through this. And to those things I cling. I know that as incomprehensible as our God is, He is faithful, loving, good, wise, and sovereign—and He will never change. God loves me. As hard as it is to grasp, understand, and even sometimes believe, in His power, grace, mercy, omnipotence, and unending love and faithfulness, this was the best, most loving thing He could have done. His timing, His ways, and His love are perfect—always.
>
> I know and believe this. I have seen God's love and faithfulness in ways I never did before. I have felt His peace, abiding presence, and grace. We truly serve an amazing God! I have never felt such grateful sorrow. I love my baby and because of God's plan for her, I love Him all the more. She brought perspective to our days and tenderness back into our hearts. God has used this to assuage our fears and give us a new heart to follow Him. No one comforts a heart as faithfully and completely as our Father.

When we go through the deepest valleys, somehow we have to believe that God knows what He's doing, and when the pain feels overwhelming, we can climb onto our heavenly Daddy's lap and cry. And He'll cry with us.

Think not thou canst sigh a sigh,
And thy Maker is not by:
Think not thou canst weep a tear,
And thy Maker is not near.

O He gives to us His joy,
That our grief He may destroy:
Till our grief is fled and gone
He doth sit by us and moan.
—WILLIAM BLAKE
"ON ANOTHER'S SORROW"
IN *Songs of Innocence*

CHILD'S PLAY

1. When you are sad or grieving, find someone who needs help more than you do. Volunteer at a homeless shelter. Tutor a child. Befriend an adult trying to learn English. Secretly take groceries to a single parent. Send an encouraging note. Go on a mission trip.
2. Name at least three areas of your life in which you can see God's hand of blessing. Thank Him for His provision.
3. When you experience a crisis, choose to believe that God has your welfare in mind. Thank Him aloud for His faithfulness and ask Him for the faith and perseverance to get through the trouble you are in. If it is severe, ask for help to get through the next minute, the next hour, or the next day. Believe that He is with you, holding you, and weeping with you.
4. During a time of crisis, find something physical to do, something that doesn't require much from you emotionally or mentally. Clean out a closet. Put pictures in albums. Make crafts. Garden. Wax your car. Also fill your life with as much beauty as you can. Spend time in nature, or bring nature to you through videos, such as those that combine music, beautiful scenery, and Scripture passages. Play praise music and sing along, even if you don't feel like it. Praise God because of who He is. He inhabits the praises of His people, and His presence will lighten your burden.

5. When you experience a crisis, call in the troops: Ask your friends, family, and church family to join you in praying about the situation. Call and request prayer from ministries that have prayer lines. If you are not in a crisis, be available for those who are.

6. Whenever you suffer or feel confused, figuratively climb onto God's lap. He understands your pain. Daddy's love will comfort you.

7. Read the book of Job. When you reach the end, remind yourself that, no matter what happens, God is sovereign. Acknowledge His right to do what He pleases with His creatures.

DADDY SAYS SO

About God's Sovereignty

At this, Job got up and tore his robe and shaved his head. Then he fell to the ground in worship and said:

"Naked I came from my mother's womb,
and naked I will depart.
The LORD gave and the LORD has taken away;
may the name of the LORD be praised."

—Job 1:20–21

The LORD said to Job:
"Will the one who contends with the Almighty correct him?
Let him who accuses God answer him!"

—Job 40:1–2

But now, LORD, what do I look for?
My hope is in you.

—Psalm 39:7

This is what the LORD says—
the Holy One of Israel, and its Maker:
Concerning things to come,
do you question me about my children,
or give me orders about the work of my hands?
It is I who made the earth
and created mankind upon it.

—Isaiah 45:11–12

About the Lord's Compassion in Our Troubles

The righteous perish,
and no one ponders it in his heart;
devout men are taken away,
and no one understands
that the righteous are taken away
to be spared from evil.
Those who walk uprightly
enter into peace;
they find rest as they lie in death.

—Isaiah 57:1–2

This I recall to my mind,
Therefore I have hope.
The LORD'S lovingkindnesses indeed never cease,
For His compassions never fail.
They are new every morning;
Great is Your faithfulness.

—Lamentations 3:21–23 NASB

Though he brings grief, he will show compassion,
so great is his unfailing love.

—Lamentations 3:32

Jesus wept.

—John 11:35

And we know that in all things God works for the good of those who love him, who have been called according to his purpose. For those God foreknew he also predestined to be conformed to the likeness of his Son, that he might be the firstborn among many brothers.

—Romans 8:28–29

Praise be to the God and Father of our Lord Jesus Christ, the Father of compassion and the God of all comfort, who comforts us in all our troubles, so that we can comfort those in any trouble with the comfort we ourselves have received from God. For just as the sufferings of Christ flow over into our lives, so also through Christ our comfort overflows.

—2 Corinthians 1:3–5

$\mathcal{D}$ADDY, YOU SCARED ME!

Childlike Reverential Fear

> With uproar hideous, first the Falls appear.
> The stunning tumult thundering on the ear
> The heaps of boiling foam, the ascending spray,
> The gulf profound, where dazzling rainbows play;
> The great o'erwhelming work of awful Time,
> In all its dread magnificence sublime,
> Rose on our view, amid a crashing roar,
> That bade us kneel and time's great God adore.
>
> —ALEXANDER WILSON
> "THE FORESTERS: A POEM DESCRIPTIVE
> OF A PEDESTRIAN JOURNEY TO THE
> FALLS OF NIAGARA," LINES 2,061–72
> (AT FIRST SIGHT OF NIAGARA FALLS, 1804)

BIG, SCARY DADDY

Sweaty from the summer heat, I awoke to familiar screaming beside me.

"Daddy! Daddy!"

"Kathy, it's okay. You just had a bad dream," I said.

I tried to put my arm around her sitting form, but she was too stiff. Wearily wishing I could go back to sleep, I tried again.

"You're okay. I'm here. It was just a bad dream."

"Daddy! Daddy!" she continued to scream, staring wildly around our room, as if she could neither see nor hear me.

I offered to go get Daddy, but she gave no response. Like a robot, Kathy got up and started walking down the hall. I jumped down to the oak floor and followed her. She stopped under the hallway light near the top of the stairs. As I peered into the blackness below and watched my sister acting so strangely, I lost all my resolve to go downstairs and wake Dad. Kathy's screaming and calling continued.

My own voice shuddered as I joined in the cry, "Daddy! Daaaddy!"

Suddenly, Kathy backed up, terrified of something in the darkness. Relieved to see my father coming up the stairs, I told her, "It's okay. Daddy's coming."

She shrieked louder and backed into the closet door, scratching at the handle trying to open it. I wondered if my sister had gone crazy. When Dad reached the top of the stairs and came face-to-face with Kathy under the light, she suddenly stopped screaming and threw her arms around his neck, sobbing. She told us later that she thought our hairy-chested Dad, who was not wearing a pajama top, was a gorilla.

DADDY'S OMNIPOTENCE

If we could see God in all His glory, He'd be much more frightening than a gorilla coming up the stairs in the dark. The prophet Ezekiel had a vision of God that so overwhelmed him that he immediately fell on his face (Ezek. 1:25–28). Isaiah, too, felt uncontrollable awe in God's presence. He panicked saying, "Woe is me, for I am ruined! Because I am a man of unclean lips, and I live among a people of unclean lips; for my eyes have seen the King, the LORD of hosts" (Isa. 6:5 NASB).

However, when Peter, James, and John saw Jesus transfigured, they apparently felt no fear at seeing His face shining like the sun and His clothes shining white with light. It didn't even seem to astonish them to see Him talking with Moses and Elijah, who had long ago left the earth. After all, they were used to seeing Jesus do amazing things. But when a luminous cloud appeared and God spoke out of the cloud, the terrified disciples fell to the ground. They didn't even look up again until Jesus touched them and calmed their fears (Matt. 17:1–8).

So many people have a deficient view of God and think of Him as only a benevolent buddy who will welcome them to heaven no matter what they believe or how they live their lives. We must remember that He is God, the frightening, all-powerful One who demands our obedience.

Facing Daddy's Wrath

Kathy and I were playing in bed instead of going to sleep, as usual. At one point our laughter got a little loud, so we tried to be quieter. We were in the middle of another game when Kathy suddenly fell silent.

"What's the matter?" I asked. "C'mon and play!" Kathy just stared at the doorway behind me.

Suddenly a hot flash of fear shot through my back. I knew. Daddy was standing at the door. I slid under the covers, afraid to look, but I knew I would have to face him.

He approached the bed. "What did I tell you girls?" He was angry, and I knew I would be punished, but like Adam, I wanted to be sure that I wasn't the only one blamed. I tried to tell him that Kathy was playing too. I was surprised to find out that he knew it already, and that he felt I had committed another atrocity by making sure my sister got in trouble with me.

Fearing anger and punishment from our earthly fathers is frightening enough. How much scarier it must be to face God as an unrepentant sinner!

Manasseh rose to the throne of Judah at age twelve and showed total defiance for God's Law. Among his many sins, he worshipped false gods, built altars to the sun, moon, and stars *inside* the temple, practiced sorcery and divination, and even killed his own son as a sacrifice to the false god Molech. According to Bible accounts, he shed a vast amount of innocent blood all across Jerusalem. He led his people to do even more evil than the nations the Lord had driven out before them (2 Kings 21:1–11, 16).

Understandably, God was angry and brought disaster on Jerusalem and Judah to punish them for their evil idolatry. He said,

> "I will wipe out Jerusalem as one wipes a dish, wiping it and turn- ing it upside down. I will forsake the remnant of my inheritance and hand them over to their enemies. They will be looted and plundered by all their foes, because they have done evil in my eyes and have provoked me to anger from the day their forefathers came out of Egypt until this day." (2 Kings 21:13–15)

What a terrifying prospect to come face-to-face with God's wrath! When we hold a benevolent view of God without remembering His justice, we don't know Him. Our heavenly Daddy is the very Power that spoke the universe into being. As we seek to develop a more inti- mate relationship with Him, our clearer understanding of His holiness should overwhelm us with reverence and fear.

TAKE OFF YOUR SHOES

Steve, Christine, and I shuffled our tired feet across a large concrete square in Istanbul, Turkey. I covered my eyes to block the bright sun- shine and examined the minaret-flanked dome of the Blue Mosque.

"You'll have to take off your shoes before you go in," Steve said.

At the entrance a man sat near a metal rack filled with dirty, worn shoes. We removed ours and paid the man. We entered the mosque in our stocking feet, overwhelmed by the unpleasant odor of thousands of unwashed feet. Sunbeams pouring through mostly blue stained- glass windows gave the large room beneath the dome a cheerful, jewel- like atmosphere. Inside a cordoned area, men knelt, their faces to the ground, worshipping without shoes. I prayed that they would come to know the true, living God and His Son, Jesus. Then I wondered why they worshipped in bare feet.

After I was back home, I did some research and found out that, just as in Moslem mosques, it is common in some cultures for people to remove their shoes, either as a sign of respect or as a reminder of their lowliness or unworthiness. Several years ago, a young friend of mine had to take off her shoes before she met the first lady of Fiji. The first lady was the only person in the room allowed to wear shoes, a reminder of her power and authority over the people in attendance.

WE STAND ON HOLY GROUND

Moses lounged on the ground near the mountain of Horeb while his sheep grazed nearby. It was hot and dusty, not unusual in this desert land. He wiped the sweat from his brow with his head covering and surveyed the landscape.

Suddenly, a flash of light on the mountainside caught his eye—fire! He jumped to his feet, anxious to protect his sheep. He knew that in this arid country, a fire could spread like wind, consuming everything in its path. But the flames seemed confined to one bush. Sparks should have ignited the bristly grass nearby, but nothing happened. The bush was in flames, but it was not consumed! *What a strange sight!* He ventured closer to take a look.

A deep voice startled him. "Moses! Moses!"

The voice came from within the burning bush. "Here I am," he answered, but he could see no one.

"Do not come any closer. Take off your sandals, for the place where you are standing is holy ground."

Moses tugged off his sandals.

"I am the God of your father, the God of Abraham, the God of Isaac and the God of Jacob."

A sudden terror overtook Moses. He didn't dare to look at God! He dropped to the ground and hid his face (see Exod. 3:1–6).

When God identified Himself, Moses understood that he was standing on a piece of earth made sacred by the presence of the living God, and it terrified him. God's holiness is frightful, and God let Moses know that His presence demanded the ultimate in reverence and respect. Evidently, that meant going barefoot.

Limited though it is, our awareness of God's supreme holiness must inspire us to humility. As our Almighty God, Creator, and Savior, He has a right to demand anything of us. We owe Him everything. So when we stand in the presence of God to worship Him, shouldn't we bare our feet, at least in spirit, and take off our self-righteousness, self-sufficiency, and pride as we acknowledge our sinfulness and vulnerability? Shouldn't we offer Him the ultimate honor and respect? Let us humble ourselves before God, for truly, when we are in His presence, we stand on holy ground.

> *The dearest idol I have known,*
> *Whate'er that idol be,*
> *Help me to tear it from thy throne,*
> *And worship only thee.*
> —WILLIAM COWPER
> "WALKING WITH GOD"

CHILD'S PLAY

1. Think of the scariest moment you have ever experienced. Now try to imagine that multiplied at least one thousand times. Just as we can't really imagine that intensity of fear, we can't begin to imagine how terrifying God is to a mere mortal.

2. The next time you pray, take off your shoes, realizing that where God is present is holy ground. Assume whatever position you feel shows Him the greatest respect—kneeling, lying facedown on the floor, standing with head bowed, etc. Then remember that God is holy, omnipotent, and scary. Worship Him as He deserves.

3. The next time you catch yourself doing something wrong, remind yourself that you are offending the same God who terrified Ezekiel, Isaiah, Peter, James, and John.

4. Think of things that are important in your life. Make a list. Then analyze your list. Are any of the things you listed in danger of

becoming idols for you (coming before God in your life)? If so, confess it. Ask God to forgive you. Then make something that represents that item, such as a picture or a model. Smash the model or tear the picture to pieces as a symbol of your release from that form of idolatry.

5. Read about tornadoes, earthquakes, hurricanes, and tsunamis. Find out which ones have been the most powerful and the most destructive. Record wind speed, force, and other statistics. Then remind yourself that God is infinitely more powerful.

6. Angle a metal bowl in the sink and turn on the water hard to make your own waterfall. If you are near a window, hold up a mirror, a piece of crystal, or a prism to the light and try to bend the light to reveal the colors of the spectrum. Then imagine you are the size of a gnat at the bottom of your sink, which for our purposes has become Niagara Falls. Rainbows have formed across the spray and the sound is so loud that you are terrified, but your awe of the beauty overwhelms you even more than your fear. What do you think you would do? Would you fall on your knees and worship the One who created it?

7. Write a poem about your first experience with something in nature that left you in awe of God's holiness.

DADDY SAYS SO

About the Fear of the Lord

> See now that I myself am He!
>   There is no god besides me.
> I put to death and I bring to life,
>   I have wounded and I will heal,
>   and no one can deliver out of my hand.
>   —Deuteronomy 32:39

The fear of the LORD is the beginning of wisdom,
And the knowledge of the Holy One is understanding.

—Proverbs 9:10 NKJV

It is a terrifying thing to fall into the hands of the living God.

—Hebrews 10:31 NASB

About God's Holiness

Who may ascend the hill of the LORD?
Who may stand in his holy place?
He who has clean hands and a pure heart,
who does not lift up his soul to an idol
or swear by what is false.

—Psalm 24:3–4

Worship the LORD in the splendor of his holiness;
tremble before him, all the earth.

—Psalm 96:9

Woe to those who go down to Egypt for help,
who rely on horses,
who trust in the multitude of their chariots
and in the great strength of their horsemen,
but do not look to the Holy One of Israel,
or seek help from the LORD.

—Isaiah 31:1

I will make known my holy name among my people Israel. I will no
longer let my holy name be profaned, and the nations will know that
I the LORD am the Holy One in Israel.

—Ezekiel 39:7

Each of the four living creatures had six wings and was covered with eyes all around, even under his wings. Day and night they never stop saying:

> "Holy, holy, holy
> is the Lord God Almighty,
> who was, and is, and is to come."
>
> —Revelation 4:8

> Who will not fear you, O Lord,
>   and bring glory to your name?
> For you alone are holy.
> All nations will come
>   and worship before you,
> for your righteous acts have been revealed.
>
> —Revelation 15:4

Part 3

INTIMACY

CHAPTER 11

CATCH ME, DADDY!

Childlike Faith

> "Jump," He whispers.
> "I'll catch you."
> But I can't see Him.
> The precipice is steep,
> the canyon deep, craggy, and wide.
>
> Fear rises and paralyzes me.
> "I can't do it."
> "But I can."
> "Abba, catch me," I cry,
> and leap.
>
> —JEANNE GOWEN DENNIS
> "TRUST"

SWING ME, DADDY!

It was almost time. Tim and Kathy stopped swinging and I froze at the top of the backyard slide. Suddenly, a deep whistle pierced through the sounds of neighborhood children and dogs at play. The whistle told us that it was five o'clock, and our dad's workday was over.

"Me first!" Kathy shouted, racing down the hill and past our house. The gate clanked against the chain-link fence just as I caught up with her. I decided to let her beat me—this time.

The three of us stationed ourselves on the sidewalk and peered up the street past our neighbors' homes. Time stood still until Timmy's scuffling feet alerted us that Daddy had rounded the corner. Kathy and I raced to beat him. Two houses away, Daddy stopped, set down his briefcase, and held out his arms. Tim jumped into them and Daddy swung him around and around. I could tell he was struggling a little to support Tim's weight.

Tim's feet had hardly touched the ground when Kathy pounced on Daddy. Small and light, she flew higher and higher with each spin. Tim and I backed away from her flying feet.

"My turn now!" I insisted.

Dad set Kathy down and took a few seconds to regain his balance. When he was ready, I got a running start and jumped. Daddy caught me with an "oomph" and I felt the thrill of flying through the air supported only by his arms.

Such was our weeknight ritual until one by one we grew too tall and too heavy for Daddy to lift. Over the years, I heard the younger children cry, "Swing me, Daddy!" and watched Dad twirling them around and around. At those times, I yearned to be small again.

Gradually, after many years of struggle, I learned to transfer my weight from my earthly daddy's arms to my heavenly Daddy's arms. It wasn't an easy transition. For a long time, I viewed myself as too sophisticated, too self-reliant to need God's support, advice, or help. I thought I was above His laws and proceeded to live for myself, in whatever way I saw fit. Life has a way of knocking us down when we get too cocky, though. Over and over, I fell flat on my face in the dirt. I'm grateful that God didn't leave me lying there. He sought me out, picked me up, cleaned me off, and then swung me around and around. At long last I felt the thrill of soaring through the air supported only by my heavenly Father's arms.

If only I could stay there all the time! Just like a child who insists that he can walk instead of being carried across a dangerous intersection, I keep falling back into the trap of thinking I can handle a few things on my own. I keep forgetting that without Jesus, I can do nothing (John 15:5), and I lose sight of who my Father really is.

THE EVERLASTING ARMS

Airplanes have always fascinated me. Every time a monstrous jetliner soars into the sky, I marvel that thin air can hold it up. Even though I enjoy flying, I can't help but wonder each time I take off whether I will arrive at my destination safely. That was especially true in 2001 after the horrors of September 11. A few months afterward, I was on a flight with dozens of empty seats and only a few fellow passengers. I had a whole row to myself. Tension had filled the airport, and most of the passengers kept silent on the plane. Israel was embattled again, and all her friends, especially U.S. citizens, were being targeted by her enemies. *That includes me, right now, and on this plane,* I thought.

I leaned against the window, watching fields, towns, and rivers pass below me—America, the beautiful. My heart ached for my country and her people, and I wondered if any place was safe. Like most Americans at the time, I was tempted to allow my fears to paralyze me, just as fear had immobilized so many others who had refused to fly. I called myself a Christian, yet at that moment I wasn't sure if I really trusted God to take care of me. After we passed over the Mississippi River, I leaned back, listening to the drone of the engines, knowing that I had to make a choice. Would I trust God even if terrorists suddenly jumped up and took over the plane? Even if I knew the plane would crash? I shuddered.

Then I reviewed what I knew about God—Creator, Savior, Shepherd, Comforter—so many aspects to His nature and yet still so fearsome and mysterious. Finally I thought, *If God really is who I believe Him to be, then He's the only One I can trust.* With a sigh, I prayed, "No matter what happens, I choose to trust You." My muscles relaxed. Others on the aircraft with me might have put their faith in airport security, the air traffic control system, and experienced pilots, but I realized that on that day and every day until God calls me home, my security, trust, and hope can be only in Him. As dangers, wars, and rumors of wars increase (Matt. 24:6; Mark 13:7), I can choose to cower in fear as life eludes me, or I can run to my heavenly Daddy, leap into His arms, and let Him transport me wherever He will. I'd rather jump on and enjoy the ride.

FRAGILE AS HUMPTY DUMPTY

It was lunchtime at the high school where I taught British literature, and the senior physics class was about to conduct its annual egg experiment. The assistant principal and three senior guys climbed onto the roof of the school while students and teachers waited below. A boy held up a small box about six-by-six-by-eight inches. "No, don't do mine first," called a girl. The box fell to the cement patio with a crunch. The girl moaned. "It broke."

One by one, eggs surrounded with bubble wrap and duct tape, or in balloon-cushioned or Styrofoam-filled boxes floated, crashed, or thudded to the ground. One egg was nestled in a stuffed animal and another in modeling clay. The students tried to guess whether the eggs inside had broken. On closer examination, they discovered slimy egg whites and yolks oozing from most of the packages. Only the stuffed animal and modeling clay eggs and one or two others survived the plunge intact.

That same day, my newlywed daughter was struggling with the stress of working two jobs, fighting possible pneumonia after a month-long illness, and cleaning a home that was in total disarray. Only five months before, she had taken a great leap of faith and married a man who had one more year of college to complete. I thought of the egg enclosed in the stuffed animal and prayed that God would wrap my fragile, grown-up little girl softly in His arms. She had jumped off a cliff with full confidence that her heavenly Father would catch her. I prayed for her to find the courage to keep looking up.

So often I find myself at the top of a figurative cliff, afraid to move ahead into what I believe is God's will. Intellectually, I know that His everlasting arms will be there to catch me, and I feel sure that He would never ask me to do something that He has not given me the power to do. But faced with that great void of the unknown, I'm still afraid to jump.

LEAPING INTO THE UNKNOWN

When I was seven, my family joined a pool with two diving boards, a "low dive" and a "high dive." I don't remember the first time I *jumped* off the low diving board, but I do recall when I graduated to diving from it. I was so afraid to go headfirst into that deep, dark water. When I finally mustered the courage, I did a belly flop and then had to overcome my embarrassment that the whole world had seen and heard it. But it was the high dive that most terrified me. It was ten or twelve feet above the water, but it might as well have been a hundred feet. I shivered at the edge of the board, hugging goose-pimpled arms, and stared at the tiny puddle below, wondering how I could ever survive the fall. More than once, I climbed back down the ladder. After a few days of teasing me mercilessly for my cowardice, my brother Danny felt sorry for me and gave me a few tips on how to overcome my fear.

The next time we went to the pool, I was determined to jump. I swam around for several minutes and kept looking at my nemesis. It loomed higher than I had remembered it. Finally, I pulled myself up the metal ladder to the pool deck and stood shivering at the back of the line of big kids and adults waiting to use the high dive.

Why can't I be alone to do this? I thought. I trembled as I waited my turn.

When I finally climbed the ladder, Dan stood down below, where I could see him. Gingerly, I crept inch by inch (literally!) to the end of the board. I turned around and started back several times. No one in line behind me complained.

"You can do it," Dan called repeatedly. Then everyone else started cheering me on. Finally, after several interminable minutes, I closed my eyes and leaped into outer space. (I now know why they call it thin air. There's nothing thick enough to grab onto.) The water hit me with a slap, but I had done it! Every time I climbed that ladder I still had to overcome the same fear, but I had joined the ranks of the "big kids," and that made all the difference.

LEAPING IN FAITH

Recently, I was in a hospital emergency room waiting for my brother, who was already being treated inside. A woman in about her late twenties sat doubled up in excruciating pain in the seat in front of me. The man with her tried to comfort her, wrapping his arm gently around her whenever the pain got worse. Finally, she went into the ladies' room. The man stood outside, obviously worried about her. I offered to go in and check on her. What I didn't tell the man was that God had been urging me to pray for the woman—aloud! That was something totally out of my comfort zone. I knew I had to obey, but it was so hard to do in front of an emergency room full of people. My insides quaked with the fear of possible rejection and embarrassment if I obeyed God—and the certainty of shame and self-condemnation if I didn't. The woman's retreat to the ladies' room had given me no more excuses.

When I went inside, she was sitting on the floor inside a stall. I heard her choking and moaning. "Oh God," she cried between sobs. "Oh God." Then she said, "Jesus, help me." That, I knew, was my cue. With her permission, I laid my hand on her shoulder and prayed for her in Jesus' name. Later, she came back into the waiting room and sat huddled in the chair again. After a few minutes, I noticed that the strain had left her face. Her body was more relaxed, and she told the man with her that her pain was going away. She said it with wonder in her voice as she looked over at me and thanked me for praying. I left her with the promise to keep praying for her, and God left me with the incredible joy and awe that comes from obeying Him and seeing Him work as a result.

RELEASING CONTROL

Sometimes our leaps of faith require much more than courage. A couple I met when I was young in my faith had just lost their only son who was about ten or twelve years old. For months, the parents, his sisters, and people all over the city had prayed for the boy's recovery, but God answered their prayers differently than they'd hoped. He said no. The mother told me that she had reached a point during her son's illness where she felt she had to give her son back to God. The boy knew he was dying and assured his parents that he was ready to be with the Lord.

"He was only lent to us for a time," she said. She admitted that even though her grief was incredible, she found peace in the midst of it. "I know that God loves my son much more than I ever could. He's in good hands."

A short time after this conversation, I knew in my heart that God was asking me to give my only child, Christine, to Him. Fear gripped me. Did it mean that my little girl was going to die too? I wrestled with God over it. "Please don't let her die," I begged in prayer. "Please!" Still, the message was clear. "I want you to give Christine back to Me."

Finally, after what must have been days of pleading, begging, and arguing, I yielded reluctantly. I told God that He had my permission to do whatever He wanted with my daughter, even if it meant that He would take her from me. As I whispered that prayer, I burst into uncontrollable sobbing, sure that I would lose her. But God has protected my daughter and raised her up into a beautiful young woman who loves and serves Him. It reminds me of when God told Abraham to sacrifice his son Isaac, but then sent an angel to stay Abraham's hand (Gen. 22:1–13). I discovered that God didn't need my permission to do His will with Christine, but I needed to give it. I needed to trust Him with her and let go enough to let Him have control of us both.

What is the Lord asking you to do today? Witness to a neighbor? Start a new job? Confess a sin to someone? Give Him your Isaac? Does the emotional precipice you're about to leap from feel far too high? It's okay. If your heavenly Daddy is calling you to jump, He'll be there to catch you. You just need to trust Him, let your feet leave the ground, and fly into His arms.

But we never can prove the delights of His love
Until all on the altar we lay;

For the favor He shows and the joy He bestows
Are for them who will trust and obey.

—JOHN H. SAMMIS
"TRUST AND OBEY"

CHILD'S PLAY

1. Are you willing to trust God to be in charge of every moment of your day? If so, tell Him. Then listen with your heart for the still, small voice of the Holy Spirit and obey.

2. How did you spend your time last week? Did God come first? Did you allow work or church activities to come before your marriage or your children? Did you leave anything important undone? Pray for God's leading and then make a list of priorities. Use that list as you plan each day.

3. Is God asking you to do something that seems far too hard? Close your eyes. Imagine that you are a child standing on the side of a pool about to jump in for the first time. You see the outstretched arms of God, your loving parent. "Jump!" He says. "I'll catch you." You're scared, but His loving arms are waiting. Muster the will to leap in obedience. Aim toward Him, and He'll catch you.

4. Who is the most precious person on earth to you? Are you willing to entrust him or her completely to God? As you pray for your loved one today, ask God to help you let go of that person enough to let God have His way, no matter what happens.

5. Think about what makes you feel secure. Is it having friends or loved ones around? Having enough money? Being successful in your career? Being able to stick to your schedule? Make a list of the people, circumstances, and things that make you feel secure or give you a greater sense of well-being. Now go through your list and, one by one, yield each thing to God. Ask Him to be your only source of security.

6. As you go through the next few months, consciously give up control of your life, one thing at a time, and give that control to God. Start each day asking God what His plan is for your day, and don't try to manipulate outcomes.

7. If you can, go swimming. Jump off the side of the pool several times, each time imagining your heavenly Father's arms waiting to catch you. Thank Him for His faithfulness.

DADDY SAYS SO

About Faith

> The eternal God is your refuge,
> and underneath are the everlasting arms.
> —Deuteronomy 33:27

> Trust in the LORD with all your heart
> and lean not on your own understanding;
> in all your ways acknowledge him,
> and he will make your paths straight.
> —Proverbs 3:5–6

He replied, "You of little faith, why are you so afraid?" Then he got up and rebuked the winds and the waves, and it was completely calm.
> —Matthew 8:26

Then Peter got down out of the boat, walked on the water and came toward Jesus. But when he saw the wind, he was afraid and, beginning to sink, cried out, "Lord, save me!"

Immediately Jesus reached out his hand and caught him. "You of little faith," he said, "why did you doubt?"
> —Matthew 14:29–31

He said to her, "Daughter, your faith has healed you. Go in peace and be freed from your suffering."
> —Mark 5:34

I tell you the truth, anyone who has faith in me will do what I have been doing. He will do even greater things than these, because I am going to the Father.

—John 14:12

In addition to all this, take up the shield of faith, with which you can extinguish all the flaming arrows of the evil one.

—Ephesians 6:16

Now faith is being sure of what we hope for and certain of what we do not see.

—Hebrews 11:1

About God's Faithfulness

He will cover you with his feathers,
and under his wings you will find refuge;
his faithfulness will be your shield and rampart.

—Psalm 91:4

For great is your love, higher than the heavens;
your faithfulness reaches to the skies.

—Psalm 108:4

For I am the LORD, your God,
who takes hold of your right hand
and says to you, Do not fear;
I will help you.

—Isaiah 41:13

Know therefore that the LORD your God is God; he is the faithful God, keeping his covenant of love to a thousand generations of those who love him and keep his commands.

—Deuteronomy 7:9

$\mathcal{D}$ADDY, YOU'RE WONDERFUL!

Childlike Humility

We wait before a window
And view an awesome sight,
A clouded glimpse of Glory,
Of Holiness and Might.

We note Love's pure reflection
In pane of shattered glass,
A never-ending story
None other could surpass.

We think we comprehend it,
And swell in pious thought
While understanding little
Of all True Love has wrought.

So trapped behind the window
We wait for open space

And keep our constant vigil
To greet Love face to face.
—JEANNE GOWEN DENNIS
"REFLECTION"

A VIEW TOO CLOSE

Our family had only three days to tour Paris, so we had to move quickly through the Musée d'Orsay. Our ten-year-old daughter made her way quickly through each gallery, seldom tarrying to study any of the paintings. When she stopped two feet in front of a large canvas, I noticed.

"What's this supposed to be?" Disgusted, she pointed to the canvas filled with small, seemingly disorganized dabs of color.

I pulled her backward until Claude Monet's image of the sunlit Rouen Cathedral appeared.

"Oh," she said, "it's a church." Only when she had stepped away from the canvas could she enjoy its jewel-like magnificence.

Like an Impressionist painting, God's handiwork often becomes clearer to us when we see it from a distance. The craggy peaks of the Colorado Rockies west of our home appear desolate up close, but viewed from farther away their grandeur is breathtaking.

God's work in us is like that too. Instead of judging our lives by the little details that might look like flaws up close, we can see more clearly after time has passed. This distance of time allows us to appreciate His exquisite technique from a vantage point that allows us to comprehend the heart of the Artist. We can recognize the beauty produced by splashes of colorful blessings contrasted with flat sections of waiting. We can even appreciate the value of hideous splotches of pain, which add the depth of shadow and help define and brighten our times of joy.

The Artist is fashioning each one of His children into a masterpiece, but as viewers of His work, we usually stand too close. Therefore, we sometimes notice the frame instead of the art—the circumstances in lieu of the results—or the areas of shadow instead of the overall picture. Only He can heal our short-sightedness by pulling us back until we can see more clearly.

Mud-Pie Vision

A man in ancient Israel had been blind from birth. No light had ever penetrated his eyes. Waiting by the roadside, he heard people approaching. They were talking about him, but he was used to the rudeness of those who could see.

One man said, "Rabbi, who sinned, this man or his parents, that he was born blind?"

A rabbi? The blind man stood up taller.

The Rabbi answered, "Neither this man nor his parents sinned, . . . but this happened so that the work of God might be displayed in his life. As long as it is day, we must do the work of him who sent me. Night is coming, when no one can work. While I am in the world, I am the light of the world."

The blind man heard the Rabbi stoop to the ground and spit. Suddenly, he felt something moist and sticky scraping across his eyes. It felt like mud. His hands went up to protect himself, but the Rabbi said, "Go, wash in the Pool of Siloam." When he did, the man was healed (see John 9:1–7).

Why mud? Why saliva? Jesus could have healed with only a word. Instead He chose to heal in a way that must have been both humbling and uncomfortable for the blind man. Yet who are we to question God's methods? He sometimes uses unpleasant things to heal our blindness too, but we must be willing to humbly submit ourselves to His wisdom, even when He chooses to clear our vision through experiences we would rather not endure.

A Closer View of Omnipotence

Steve called me from downstairs. "Quick, they're talking about Palm Coast."

"Who? What?"

"On the news. Hurry!"

When I stumbled into the family room, footage of flames, smoke, and burning forests and homes shocked me into silence. A wildfire that had been burning for several days had devoured hundreds of acres and several neighborhoods and was heading into new areas, including the one where my parents lived. I tried calling them, but all the circuits were busy.

Finally, after agonizing hours, I learned that they had evacuated safely. When the fire was contained, they discovered that their house had survived, but the flames had come within two miles of it. Firefighters had put forth monumental effort to get the fire under control, but they were helpless to prevent all the destruction left in its path.

Humans are powerless to prevent the devastation caused by natural disasters such as fires, earthquakes, hurricanes, tsunamis, floods, and tornadoes. We marvel at the damage to life and property that they cause, and we wonder at the phenomenal power behind such events. If we experience a disaster firsthand, our fear and pain remind us of our vulnerability—and our need for God.

As a result of human sinfulness, natural tragedies are part of our imperfect world,[1] but their incredible force attests to the awesome power of God, the Creator of earth, wind, waves, fire, and water. Our inability to stop natural catastrophes reminds us that He *is* God and enormously more powerful than we can imagine.

Yet that same all-powerful God humbled Himself, even to death on a cross, to pay for the sin that has wrought such havoc on the world.

A Clearer View of Love

One summer day, I went to the backyard to pick cherries. As I approached the tree, finches and robins flitted to higher branches to continue feasting on the fruit. While filling my bowl, I noticed that the tree's bark looked different. Amber jewels glistened in the morning sunlight, forming a sap necklace around a main branch. The leaking sap indicated that underneath the tree's bark-skin—deep inside—insect marauders stole away its life, eating away like a slow-moving cancer. Even trees suffer the consequences of sin, because thousands of years ago a young woman believed a lie.

When Adam and Eve first sinned (see Gen. 3:1–6), the serpent twisted its coils around the Creator's masterpiece, and creation groaned. Everything was affected. Birds now fight in midair. Insects take chunks out of roses. Animals eat one another. Diseases smother, decay, and wither plants, animals, and people. Natural disasters and wars wreak devastation. And death steals our loved ones away from us—for now.

From the beginning, the Artist planned to redeem His masterpiece from the clutches of the serpent. So in time, the Artist became Eve's offspring—God in human flesh—and paid the price of freedom.

What incredible love! God made this glorious earth and created humankind to enjoy it and to be His intimate friends. His love is so complete that when our sin spoiled His masterpiece, He took the punishment, paid the penalty, and began its restoration (John 1:1–3; 10:11). In His mercy, God heals the eyes of our souls so that we can see through evil's distortions and view glimpses of the pure image of His glory as we wait for His return.

A REVERSE IMAGE

It was much earlier than my usual time to leave. As I ventured outside into the cool predawn air, everything appeared to be painted in shades of gray and black. Indistinguishable shapes melted into one another, seemingly covered in a gauzelike drape, until gradually the sky began to lighten. Grays turned to muted tones, and then suddenly the sky blushed azure, gold, and magenta, splashing color across the landscape. I inhaled the dew-kissed breeze, savored the visual feast of morning, and poured out my praise to the Artist.

In the same way that a landscape becomes more discernible with sunlight, our image of God grows clearer as our eyes grow used to His light. When God opens our eyes through grace, we understand that our former view of the Creator and His work was a reverse image, like a photographic slide turned backward. Just as leafless trees and shrubs in winter appear dead while they rest and store energy that will burst forth into springtime growth, our lives are not what we would naturally expect. True freedom is not being able to do what we want, whenever we want. Freedom is found in freely choosing to submit our wills to the One who has given us His grace. To gain life, we have to die to ourselves. To flourish, we have to suffer. To press on through pain and hardship, we must admit our weakness and lean only on His strength.

As we mature in our knowledge of God, we suddenly realize that humanity's lofty intelligence, theories, skills, and ideas amount to little when compared to God's infinite knowledge. Nevertheless, we are the crowning glory of His creation.

HIS IMAGE IN US

God made mankind in His own image (Gen. 1:27), and because His image is implanted in us so strongly, we feel compelled to imitate Him. As children of our creative and eternal Father, we try to recreate life and beauty, and we long to accomplish something of lasting value. So we have children, decorate our homes, grow gardens, and build human versions of mountains in concrete and steel. We give and receive love. We express ourselves through writing, art, drama, music, and dance.

What makes us imagine that we can improve on a mountain vista bursting with sights, scents, and sounds by rendering it in a painting, describing it in poetry, or interpreting it in a symphony? Our cultural developments, art, music, and literature pale to dull gray in the shadow of God's creativity. He is so unbelievably great, so unfathomably above us that the best that humanity has to offer simply fades to nothingness.

Even though our best efforts can't come close to the originals, God must be pleased by our attempts to imitate, describe, and interpret the beauty He created. Artists, after all, incorporate heartfelt messages into their art, and the viewer's response completes the communication.

Through His art, God tells us who He is. He invites us to know Him better and to bask in His reflection until more and more of His image shines out through us. Even before we have Jesus in our lives, we bear a likeness to our heavenly Father, but it is only after His Holy Spirit starts working in us that we begin to resemble His holiness and perfection. It is only as we humble ourselves like children in the presence of the most wonderful One of all that we can grow more and more into His likeness.

> *Holy God, holy God,*
> *Through shaded eyes we see*
> *Glimpses of Your holiness,*
> *Your love, and purity.*
>
> *Holy God, holy God,*
> *What power and majesty!*
> *Oh how great, how wonderful,*
> *How holy You must be!*
> JEANNE GOWEN DENNIS
> "HOLY GOD"

CHILD'S PLAY

1. Think about the experiences in your life that were difficult. Write down your thoughts about those situations. Looking back at them now, can you see how God incorporated those problems into His perfect plan for your life? How did you grow from them? What did you learn that helps you now?
2. Play Blind Man's Bluff. As you are wearing the blindfold, remember that only God can see everything—our past, our present, and our future. Then wear the blindfold as you pray alone. Tell God that wherever He leads you, you will trust Him instead of trusting your own unclear vision.
3. The Bible describes the earth as God's footstool. Imagine yourself, right where you are, as a miniscule speck at the base of the footstool. Look up at the throne. How humble do you feel now? Give God the glory and praise He deserves.

4. Go to an art gallery or anywhere you can see original works of art. Find a piece you really like. Then get close and look at the details. View them as individual elements and not as part of the whole. Do you find some of them unattractive? Dull? Boring? Now back up and observe how those elements contribute to the beauty of the painting. Then thank God for everything you've gone through, because you can be assured that He'll use it for good. Memorize Romans 8:28–29.

5. Look at some aspect of creation and write down the message you think God is speaking to you through it. Then read Psalms 19 and 98.

6. Find a scene in nature that inspires you with its beauty. Try to paint it, write about it, or describe it to someone else. Is your visual, written, or verbal description adequate? Will that make you stop trying to imitate God's artwork? I hope not. Hang your artwork or writing on your refrigerator as a reminder that you are a child of the Artist, imitating one of His incredible masterpieces. Feel His pleasure at your efforts.

7. Make mud pies and thank God for using even the dirtiest, grossest things in life to open your eyes to His love.

DADDY SAYS SO

About God's Image

You cannot see my face, for no one may see me and live.

—Exodus 33:20

Now we see but a poor reflection as in a mirror; then we shall see face to face. Now I know in part; then I shall know fully, even as I am fully known.

—1 Corinthians 13:12

About Us Reflecting God's Image

And we, who with unveiled faces all reflect the Lord's glory, are being transformed into his likeness with ever-increasing glory, which comes from the Lord, who is the Spirit.

—2 Corinthians 3:18

Dear friends, now we are children of God, and what we will be has not yet been made known. But we know that when he appears, we shall be like him, for we shall see him as he is.

—1 John 3:2

About Humility

You save the humble,
> but your eyes are on the haughty to bring them low.

—2 Samuel 22:28

When I shut up the heavens so that there is no rain, or command locusts to devour the land or send a plague among my people, if my people, who are called by my name, will humble themselves and pray and seek my face and turn from their wicked ways, then will I hear from heaven and will forgive their sin and will heal their land.

—2 Chronicles 7:13–14

You save the humble
but bring low those whose eyes are haughty.

—Psalm 18:27

He guides the humble in what is right
and teaches them his way.

—Psalm 25:9

I praise you because I am fearfully and wonderfully made;
  your works are wonderful,
I know that full well.

—Psalm 139:14

For the LORD takes delight in his people;
  he crowns the humble with salvation.

—Psalm 149:4

"Has not my hand made all these things,
  and so they came into being?"
  declares the LORD.
"This is the one I esteem:
  he who is humble and contrite in spirit,
  and trembles at my word."

—Isaiah 66:2

Humble yourselves, therefore, under God's mighty hand, that he
may lift you up in due time.

—1 Peter 5:6

$\mathcal{D}$ADDY, I WANT TO BE JUST LIKE YOU

Childlike Imitation

O to be like Thee! Blessed Redeemer,
This is my constant longing and prayer;
Gladly I'll forfeit all of earth's treasures,
Jesus, Thy perfect likeness to wear.

O to be like Thee! Full of compassion,
Loving, forgiving, tender, and kind;
Helping the helpless, cheering the fainting,
Seeking the wand'ring sinner to find.

Oh! to be like Thee, lowly in spirit,
Holy and harmless, patient and brave;
Meekly enduring cruel reproaches,
Willing to suffer, others to save.

—THOMAS O. CHISHOLM
"O TO BE LIKE THEE!"

Just Like Daddy

On our first day of vacation, I wakened to find two-year-old Christine standing on a chair in front of a hotel mirror beside her dad. Both of them had shaving cream on their faces.

"I'm shaving with Daddy," she announced matter-of-factly as she copied his movements using the smooth "razor" Steve had fashioned for her from a cup.

It reminded me of a few days before, when I had discovered Christine admiring herself in the mirror with my high heels over her socks and most of a tube of lipstick on her mouth and cheeks. Our little daughter wanted to be just like us.

As Christians, we want to be just like Jesus. We hope that as we grow in our relationship with Him, we will eventually look into the mirror of our souls and see His image shining back at us.

The Spitting Image

One snowy day in January I was watching my neighbor's two nieces. As we sat at the kitchen table together, three-year-old Noelle squeezed her cheeks between chubby hands, trying to push them toward her eyes.

"I can't see my face," she finally announced, as if it were a new revelation. "Can you see your face?"

"No, I can't," I said.

"Only I can see my face in a mirror. Can you see your face in a mirror?"

I assured her that I could.

What a surprise it must be for a child to first discover that, although she can feel her face, she can't see it. Even when she looks in a mirror, it takes a measure of faith for her to believe that the face staring back at her is her own.

In the same way, it is a revelation for believers when we grasp that we have a true image we can't see. Only by looking in the mirror that is Jesus Christ can we begin to understand it. As believers, we wear His image, but we are far from being just like Him. Whatever good may reside in us is nothing compared with Christ's perfection.

When we express a desire to be like Jesus, we may have romantic ideas about how holy we will become. But becoming like Jesus involves so much more than we can fathom. "The Son is the radiance of God's glory and the exact representation of his being, sustaining all things by his powerful word" (Heb. 1:3). Jesus' perfection is so far beyond our reach that it seems ludicrous even to consider trying to be like Him. Jesus is pure. Jesus is good. Jesus is all powerful, and we're not.

One of my favorite paintings depicts a little boy trying to follow his daddy by putting his small feet into his father's much larger footprints in the snow. Looking at the painting, we know that the little boy has a long way to go before he can duplicate his father's steps, yet just the act of following his dad each day will bring him closer to his goal.

Our feet will never be able to fill the footprints Jesus left; yet He still asks us to follow Him. And so we shave with a smooth razor and don His too-large shoes, mimicking His every movement as we learn more each day what it means to be like Jesus.

LIKE FATHER, LIKE CHILD

Christine was sitting on Granddaddy's lap. She was just old enough to have noticed that his hand and forearm had been amputated.

"Granddaddy, what happened to your hand?"

He explained that it got hurt and had to be cut off.

"Will it grow back?"

"No."

Her look of compassion and concern deepened. "Does it hurt?" Without waiting for an answer she said, "I'm going to kiss it better." She smacked a kiss on the tip of his stump. "There. Does that feel better?" She hopped down. "You're okay, Granddaddy. It's all better now."

Children often show compassion like Christ's. Toddlers and young children will rush to the aid of another child who has fallen or gotten hurt. Some will even reach out to hurting adults as if they were adults themselves.

Jesus exemplified compassion everywhere He went, healing the sick, feeding the hungry, and being kind to those caught in slavery to sin. Sometimes He helped even without being asked, as when he raised a woman's only son back to life (Luke 7:11–15). But compassion like His is hard to find.

Standing on our neighbor's lawn without coats in thirty-degree weather, we watched smoke billowing from our home as it burned. All around us, people who lived in the apartments near our house stood at a distance, watching us as if we were images on a TV screen. Perhaps the neighbors were in as much shock as we were or felt too uncomfortable to approach us, for they didn't seem to notice our need for help. No one talked to us or offered blankets, coats, or hot drinks.

Sometimes when we encounter suffering people, we would like to offer assistance or sympathy but we hesitate for fear that our efforts might be misunderstood or rejected. Without God's help, we can't love the unlovely or effectively give comfort to those who grieve, but when God fills us with His love and we allow Him to work through us, we can find the courage and wisdom to show true compassion, even in uncomfortable situations.

STANDING IN

After waiting several days for a cut to heal, a three-year-old girl would finally be allowed to go swimming with her five-year-old sister and six-year-old brother. But she had to make her bed and pick up her room first. Mommy had said so before she left. When the family's nanny reminded the child that she had to do her chores, the girl folded her arms and firmly said no.

The nanny reminded her two more times. "If you don't clean your room, then you can't go swimming."

The child would not budge.

"Okay, then you can't go swimming."

Suddenly the girl said, "I go make my bed now."

The nanny followed her. "I'm proud of you for making your bed, but you still can't go swimming, because you disobeyed me three times." The child's brother was shocked. "But she's doing it. Why can't she go swimming?"

"Your sister disobeyed me three times. She needs to be punished. She will have to sit by the pool while you swim."

The boy mulled it over, devastated that his little sister had to miss the fun she had been looking forward to so much. "Can I take her place?"

The nanny's heart melted at his compassionate request, and she praised the boy for his kindness. "You know, that's exactly what Jesus did for us. He took our punishment when He died on the cross."

Because of the brother's love for his sister, the nanny decided to show mercy, just as God showed us mercy. The girl got to go swimming after she sat out for a little while.

The boy's childlike heart understood his sister's suffering. He was willing to pay the cost for her disobedience. Emulating Jesus often requires sacrifice, and it always requires us to forgive others, just as Jesus forgave us even as He hung on the cross in our place.

ALWAYS FORGIVING

Forgiveness seems to be one of the hardest gifts of all to give, no matter what our age. Yet we must forgive if we are to become like Jesus. It's easy to forgive little offenses, but what about the ones that leave large wounds or are never completely resolved? How can God expect people to forgive those who have killed their child, stolen their husband, maimed their body, or betrayed their deepest trust? How can God expect us to forgive such grievous offenses? There are no easy answers to these questions. Our understanding extends only to the borders of our knowledge and experience; God's understanding is infinite. Since He commands us to forgive others, it must be important. In fact, Jesus said that it is essential for our own forgiveness (Matt. 6:14–15). In addition, when we hold on to hurts and cannot forgive those who harm us, our unforgiveness eats away at us like a disease. It damages us more than it could possibly harm those who hurt us.

So how can we forgive the unforgivable? We can't. Only God's love working in us can do that. If we give Him our willingness to obey, we can forgive, as difficult and painful as it is. The pain may even keep resurfacing, but as we continue to choose forgiveness in God's strength, then we'll gradually recover from the disease of unforgiveness, and we will have become a little more like our heavenly Daddy and our heavenly Brother, Jesus.

SHARING HIS SUFFERING

The television showed a young Sudanese boy who had been mutilated, enslaved, and abused after his parents and friends had been murdered and his village burned to the ground—simply because they believed in Jesus Christ.

Christians all over the world are being persecuted and killed for their faith. Although Christian beliefs are ridiculed in America and discussion of them is disallowed in most public forums, most Americans suffer only little prickles of disagreement, not the painful thorns of persecution. Perhaps it is how we handle the prickles, though, that will determine whether or not we will persevere when the thorns come. Growing to be more like God may require us to share in Jesus' suffering and shame. Most of us have never had to claim Jesus as our Savior while looking down the barrel of a gun. If faced with that choice, would we have the faith, strength, and conviction we need to give up our lives for the name of Jesus? Do we even have what it takes to give up our everyday lives to God's purposes?

PURE AND GOOD

When I was ten, our family was picnicking by a beautiful, clear creek. We older kids explored along the rocky shore, took off our shoes and socks, and waded in the cold water while Mom situated herself and the baby in the shade. I was just about to show Mike how to scoop up water for a drink when Dad stopped me.

"The water isn't clean enough to drink."

He couldn't have shocked me more if he'd said a spaceship had just landed on the other side of the park. That creek had some of the clearest water I had ever seen. In the mugginess of a Maryland summer, its fresh coldness just begged to be tasted, but I had to let it pour through my fingers. Dad explained that bugs in the water could make us sick. Other than a few water striders scooting on the surface and some water beetles swimming underneath, I couldn't see anything.

"I'll make sure he doesn't drink any bugs," I said.

Dad laughed and explained that the bugs were microscopic—too small to see with our eyes. I had never heard of bugs smaller than we could see, and I was not convinced that someone with good eyesight couldn't spot them anyway. True to form, I took that as a challenge and scooped up handful after handful of water searching for microscopic "bugs," which of course I never found.

Even though the creek water looked perfect, it was filled with impurities, just like people who appear to be good. None of us is good, nor can we be. Jesus said that only God is good (Mark 10:18). Even the best Christians fail to measure up to His standard of perfection. We gossip. We complain. We turn our eyes away from the poor. We enjoy entertainment that flaunts disobedience to God's commandments and dishonors His name. Yet Jesus told us to be perfect as our heavenly Father is perfect (Matt. 5:48). As an example to us, He lived out that perfection when He was on earth, staying pure in every way while fighting the same temptations we face (Heb. 4:15).

Although Jesus didn't have television, movies, or the World Wide Web, He surely passed by loose women trying to lure customers. Satan must have tempted Him to spout foul language, covet the belongings or successes of others, and let His anger fly out of control. When He saw Roman soldiers mistreating and killing His people, He must have been tempted to want revenge. Still, Jesus stayed pure. Yet even as He shunned sin, He welcomed sinners as friends and told them to "go and sin no more."

Have you ever seen a small child try to walk in his daddy's boots? The child can't do it. But if the dad holds the boots on and helps the child, he can walk. If we are to follow in Jesus' footsteps, we will have to wear His boots with His help. We have the hope of eternal life *only* because Jesus imparts His own perfection and purity to us (see Rom. 4:23–25; Gal. 3:27; Heb. 10:5–23). Remembering that it's His goodness, and His alone, that overcomes our imperfection, let's imitate Him as best we can. As we let His goodness and power rule in our lives, His image will shine clearer in the mirror of our souls.

> *O to be like Thee! O to be like Thee,*
> *Blessed Redeemer, pure as Thou art!*
> *Come in Thy sweetness, come in Thy fullness*
> *Stamp Thine own image deep on my heart.*
> —THOMAS O. CHISHOLM
> "O TO BE LIKE THEE!"

CHILD'S PLAY

1. When you hear the daily news today, try to understand God's heart for the world, for those who suffer and for those who are trapped in slavery to sin. When you hear about something that grieves the heart of God, cry with Him.

2. In a situation from #1, pray about how God would have you help to make a difference. Can you volunteer? Share your faith? Write a letter? Donate money? Write a letter to the editor or news anchor? Even if you cannot do anything else, be faithful to pray about the situation.

3. This week, give up something you want to do, such as watching a movie. Use that time to bless someone in need.

4. Read each of the Gospels one at a time. As you do, take notes about Jesus' characteristics and the ways He demonstrated them. Figuratively, sit at His feet; become a student of His words, actions, and character. The better you know what the Bible teaches

about Jesus, the better you will know Him, and the easier it will be to imitate Him.

5. Take some of your notes from #4 and think of ways you can imitate those characteristics in your own life.

6. You may have painful memories from your past or hurts that have not healed. Make a list of every offense that still bothers you— times when you were mistreated, lied about, abused, and so on. Read Psalms 23; 31; 54; 138; Matthew 5:44; and Luke 6:27–38. Pray for God to help you forgive those who have hurt you. Then choose to forgive each offense on your list, crossing it out as a sign of closure. Destroy the paper. The quicker you forgive, the sooner you will find healing and the closer you will draw to the Daddy who forgives us all.

7. Watch for qualities of Jesus in little children. As you find examples of little children behaving as Jesus might, write them down in a notebook or prayer journal under headings such as "Kindness," "Self-sacrifice," etc. Reread them periodically as inspiration for yourself.

DADDY SAYS SO

About Jesus as Our Example

Father, if you are willing, take this cup from me; yet not my will, but yours be done.

—Luke 22:42

Jesus said, "Father, forgive them, for they do not know what they are doing."

—Luke 23:34

Do not be conquered by evil, but conquer evil with good.

—Romans 12:21 HCSB

Let us fix our eyes on Jesus, the author and perfecter of our faith, who for the joy set before him endured the cross, scorning its shame, and sat down at the right hand of the throne of God. Consider him who endured such opposition from sinful men, so that you will not grow weary and lose heart.

—Hebrews 12:2–3

About Becoming Like God

But I tell you: Love your enemies and pray for those who persecute you, that you may be sons of your Father in heaven. . . . Be perfect, therefore, as your heavenly Father is perfect.

—Matthew 5:44–45, 48

Be careful not to do your "acts of righteousness" before men, to be seen by them. If you do, you will have no reward from your Father in heaven.

—Matthew 6:1

If anyone would come after me, he must deny himself and take up his cross and follow me. For whoever wants to save his life will lose it, but whoever loses his life for me and for the gospel will save it.

—Mark 8:34–35

Be merciful, just as your Father is merciful.

—Luke 6:36

Jesus replied, "If anyone loves me, he will obey my teaching."

—John 14:23

Be imitators of God, therefore, as dearly loved children and live a life of love, just as Christ loved us and gave himself up for us as a fragrant offering and sacrifice to God.

But among you there must not be even a hint of sexual immorality, or of any kind of impurity, or of greed, because these are improper for God's holy people.

—Ephesians 5:1–3

Each of you should look not only to your own interests, but also to the interests of others.

—Philippians 2:4

Religion that God our Father accepts as pure and faultless is this: to look after orphans and widows in their distress and to keep oneself from being polluted by the world.

—James 1:27

But just as he who called you is holy, so be holy in all you do; for it is written: "Be holy, because I am holy."

—1 Peter 1:15–16

Dear friends, since God so loved us, we also ought to love one another.

—1 John 4:11

$\mathcal{L}$OOK OUT, DADDY, HERE I COME!

Childlike Freedom

I like to walk with bare feet.
The cool linoleum reminds me of childhood
summers when shoes were reserved for
Sunday School and out-of-town company.

I like the softness and sponginess
of a carpet beneath my feet,
like a pillow under my head.

Outside, I like to feel soft clover,
bermuda grass, mud, or warm sand
between my toes and on my soles.

And in the winter I prop cold feet
in front of the fire and let it warm me
like a cup of hot chocolate.

I like to jump, skip and run with a freedom
that is harnessed by shoes,
then in sweet abandon and praise,
dance barefoot before my creator.[1]
                                        —LOUISE TUCKER JONES
                                        "DANCING BAREFOOT"

FREEDOM TO BE YOURSELF

In fourth grade, I was part of the popular crowd, the smart kids who looked down their noses at others because they weren't as successful academically as we were. By fifth grade, though, things had changed. My friends developed interests that I cared nothing about—in particular, boys and cheerleading. I began to feel like an outsider.

Instead of developing my own interests, I tried to squeeze back into the group's restructured mold so that I could still be one of "them." So, when cheerleading tryouts were announced, I decided to give it a try. I didn't exactly understand what cheerleaders did, since I had never been to a game, but my best friend was trying out, so I did too. She intently worked on her own skills, but no matter how I tried, I could not figure out what I was supposed to do. Needless to say, I felt foolish at tryouts and was not surprised when my friend made the squad and I didn't.

From that point on, she spent most of her time talking about boys and growing in her other friendships. One last time, I tried to ignore our growing differences and let myself be pressed into naming two boys that I liked. I had to think hard, but eventually confided to her the names of two boys who always seemed polite and kind to others. She and her other friends ridiculed me for my supposed crushes, because I had made my choices from outside their select group of "cute" boys.

Even with my friend's betrayal, I longed for things to be as they used to be, so I tried on her popular identity. One day I saw three boys from my class playing baseball in the field behind my house. I imagined myself a cheerleader and put on a sweater, skirt, knee socks, and tennis shoes and hid in the bushes, watching them from a distance. I thought up cheers and wondered which boy I should shout for. Before I made a fool of myself, I realized that the cheerleading identity was not for me and hurried home to change.

I suppose that my slow progress in discovering my own personality took its toll. Soon my best friend and the others from our crowd stopped associating with me altogether. They even made up chants to taunt me at recess. After months of this abuse, I finally wandered over to the part of the playground where the other girls played—those I had always considered beneath me, even though I didn't know them very well. A group of girls were jumping rope, which my old group of friends no longer considered cool.

As I watched the other girls, a distant memory forced itself to the surface of my mind. *I used to like jump rope.*

Just then, a girl walked over and asked, "Would you like to play?"

Her acceptance of me was like a ray of sunshine in the midst of a storm. I joined them and soon found out that I had a lot in common with this group of girls. They became my good friends, and I finally found the freedom to be myself.

In our relationship with Jesus, we have the freedom to be who God created us to be. When we allow Him to mold our unique gifts and talents for His glory, we find fulfillment as we give Him pleasure. But we have to be sure to follow where He leads and not let other people or circumstances distract or discourage us.

FREEDOM TO FOLLOW

It would be my first ballet recital, and I was to play one of the horses. As I donned my mane headdress and my sparkling white and gold leotard and tights, I reviewed our teacher's instructions. "Make sure you prance far enough forward to make room for the horses behind you."

I recalled the dress rehearsal when the girls at the end of the two lines crowded into a crooked huddle at the back of our small stage. I felt keenly the heavy responsibility of being the first in line, and, consequently, the closest to the audience on my side of the stage.

The performance went well, and we were going into our final formation. We pranced and pawed the air as we formed two angled lines. *Go up far enough,* I told myself, hopping with pointed toes toward the audience. I glanced across the stage to the leader of the line on the opposite side. We appeared to be aligned. The music ended and we took our final pose. The audience clapped. We bowed. Then the curtain closed—behind me. I was left alone to face a laughing crowd of spectators. At once mortified, I turned my back to the audience and desperately tried to pull the multilayered curtain aside to escape. Finally, after what felt like an hour to me, my teacher realized what had happened. She opened the curtain from the side and pulled me behind it.

Though I had followed my teacher's instructions, it appeared to the audience that I had failed. For weeks I was identified, to my shame, as "the horse who got stuck in front of the curtain."

Nowadays, little ballerinas can depend on pieces of tape on the stage to help them know where to go, but I had only a verbal instruction. I was left to judge for myself how far forward was far enough. I found out later that the other line leader scrambled behind the curtain just before it closed. She too had gone too far forward.

Sometimes following God feels just as uncertain as a stage without tape guides. We can't see where He's leading us. We might feel as if we're standing out in front of everyone looking foolish, because no one else heard our instructions.

Other people have their own opinions about what we should do, where we should go, and when we should do it. Although it's important to heed wise counsel, the final authority in our lives must be the Lord. After we seek His will through prayer and Scripture, we need to rest in the knowledge that He is in charge and will make things right in the end. We must embrace the freedom to follow Him one step at a time, even when the path doesn't make sense to us. He can see where we're going, even when we can't.

The Freedom of Faith

My sister Christine, her husband Jim, and their five young children were on the way home from Grandma and Grandpa's one dark evening. Lightning flashed and thunder crashed violently around them as the wind buffeted their van. The road was slippery, and a radio announcer reported that a tornado had touched down within a mile of their location. Concerned for their family's safety, the parents were discussing whether to turn back or try to find shelter. They knew the tornado could be heading in any direction, and were in a quandary about where to go.

Then a calm little voice floated up from the back of the van. "Don't worry, Mommy, God's still with us." It was five-year-old Tommy who put everything back into perspective.

They continued toward home. Outside, the elements roared, but inside the van, peace reigned. It was the peace that only God can give, the peace that no one really understands. It can come in the midst of the worst of stormy weather, or it can take hold of us gradually as we progressively exchange fear for courage.

Freedom from Fear

I was watching my daughter Christine play with various toys in the tub when Steve arrived home from a trip. After he greeted us, he said, "I brought you a present, Christine." Then he threw something small and black across the room into the water. Christine bolted out of the tub onto the rug, screaming. Steve laughed and picked the item out of the water while I wrapped her in a towel to comfort her.

Steve held up the gift. "Look, it's a plastic spider. Isn't it cool?" (Only a man could imagine that a three-year-old girl would get excited about a plastic spider!) Finally I convinced Steve that throwing a realistic-looking, oversized arachnid into the tub without first telling the child that it was a toy had not been a good idea. He placed the spider on the counter and we tried to calm her down enough to finish her bath.

For the next two weeks, I observed our daughter staring at that plastic spider every time she went by it. Each day she would force herself to move closer to it until one day she got near enough to touch it. I watched as she reached out her hand and pulled it back several times. Finally, she touched the spider. Two days later, she was playing with it just like any other toy. I was amazed that at such a young age she had forced herself to persevere until she overcame her fear.

As Christians, we have the Lord to help us conquer our fears, but just like my daughter, we may have to force ourselves to muster the courage to face them head on. God gives us the strength, but we have to act on it. God also gives us gifts that we don't always recognize as gifts, such as His laws that may at first seem to bind us, but in reality set us free.

THE FREEDOM OF SUBMISSION

My daughter once told me that the scariest thing a parent can tell a child about making a decision is, "I'll tell you what I think, but then you're on your own." Children need the boundaries parents give them, not only so they will know how to behave, but also to make them feel secure.

We need boundaries too—the boundaries God has set for us. In the book of Romans, the apostle Paul pointed out that no matter what we do, we will be in bondage to something—either to sin, if we insist on going our own way, or to righteousness if we follow Jesus (Rom. 6:19). He wrote:

> For when you were slaves of sin, you were free from allegiance to righteousness. And what fruit was produced then from the things you are now ashamed of? For the end of those things is death. But now, since you have been liberated from sin and become enslaved to God, you have your fruit, which results in sanctification [or holiness]—and the end is eternal life! (Romans 6:20–22 HCSB)

Slavery to sin ends in death. Slavery to God results in freedom—freedom to approach His holy throne and call Him "Daddy"; freedom to become who we were created to be; and freedom to live, laugh, love, and rejoice. We can do all these things, because we know that no matter how difficult our life on earth becomes, nothing can separate us from the love of Jesus (Rom. 8:35–39), and our end is eternal joy with Him.

FREEDOM FOR PASSION

The October air was cool and the sun bright as Mom, Dad, Steve, and I walked down the wooden steps over the sand dunes to the beach. Steve was carrying three-year-old Christine, and as we neared the water, he set her down.

"Feel the ocean, Christine," he said, splashing the water toward her. Then he placed her hand in it.

She didn't like its coldness, but more than that, something else had her attention. The vast expanse of sand and the call of the wind beckoned her, so she started running. As fast as she could, she darted along the endless shoreline, elated with her newfound freedom. From that day until she was at least six, every time we took her to the beach, Christine ran with the wind, like a passionate horse, and the adults had an increasingly hard time catching up with her.

That's the kind of excitement our Christian lives can have, if we answer the call of the Holy Spirit with the exuberance of a child racing along the seashore. A life lived in close fellowship with God is a fulfilled one. When we obey—even though He may ask us to do things we do not want to do—we feel satisfaction, peace, and joy, and sometimes even ecstasy, as we begin to grasp His incredible love for us.

FREEDOM TO PRAISE

Tonya is big for her age, and much larger than her mental age. Everyone at church knows who she is, and they understand that she is a little different. One day during the service, Tonya was overcome by the music and her desire to worship God. In the middle of a song, she rose from her seat, went to the center of the aisle, and danced her message of love to God.

I wonder what those watching her felt. Embarrassment? Amusement? Envy? How wonderful it would be to experience the freedom that would allow us to be everything God created us to be, no matter what anyone else thought. How blessed we would be if we could learn to be like Tonya, expressing our love freely and openly to God as we worship Him with all our hearts.

> *Have Thine own way, Lord!*
> *Have Thine own way!*
> *Hold o'er my being absolute sway!*
> *Fill with Thy Spirit till all shall see*
> *Christ only, always, living in me!*
> —ADELAIDE A. POLLARD
> "HAVE THINE OWN WAY, LORD"

CHILD'S PLAY

1. If it's okay to shout for players on a sports field and performers on stage, then it should be okay, somewhere, to shout out our love for God. Make up a cheer for God. Choose an aspect of His character, an event in the Bible, or a way that He has blessed you. Write about it. Make it rhyme. Then make up motions to go with it. Now jump and shout!

2. Think of something you used to enjoy doing as a child, something that would not be considered "cool" now by older children. It could be jumping rope, hopping on one foot, whistling between two pieces of grass, or whatever you like. Whatever it is, do it now as a reminder that God made you who you are and you are free to be yourself.

3. Try to think of a time when you tried to do God's will, but in the eyes of others, you failed. Draw a picture of that situation with

you standing alone in front of everyone. Then draw Jesus standing beside you.

4. Buy a plastic spider or make one from clay. Keep it as a reminder that, even if it takes you several weeks or months, you can conquer any fear with God's help.

5. Find someone to play with you. Draw a circle with chalk on the driveway or pavement. Bounce a ball to each other, making sure that it stays inside the circle. As you play, talk about the boundaries God has provided for us and how they protect us.

6. Run like the wind, spin like a top, swing your arms and shout, or do something else that makes you feel free. Think of it as a symbol of the freedom you have in Jesus and the elation that comes from a close relationship with God.

7. Put on your favorite praise music and dance barefoot before the Lord.

DADDY SAYS SO

About Freedom

> I will walk about in freedom,
> for I have sought out your precepts.
> —Psalm 119:45

To the Jews who had believed him, Jesus said, "If you hold to my teaching, you are really my disciples. Then you will know the truth, and the truth will set you free."

—John 8:31–32

Jesus replied, "I tell you the truth, everyone who sins is a slave to sin. Now a slave has no permanent place in the family, but a son belongs to it forever. So if the Son sets you free, you will be free indeed."

—John 8:34–36

For we know that our old self was crucified with Him in order that sin's dominion over the body may be abolished, so that we may no longer be enslaved to sin.

—Romans 6:6 HCSB

But thank God that, although you used to be slaves of sin, you obeyed from the heart that pattern of teaching you were entrusted to, and having been liberated from sin, you became enslaved to righteousness.

—Romans 6:17–18 HCSB

But now we have been released from the law, since we have died to what held us, so that we may serve in the new way of the Spirit and not in the old letter of the law.

—Romans 7:6 HCSB

Therefore, no condemnation now exists for those in Christ Jesus, because the Spirit's law of life in Christ Jesus has set you free from the law of sin and of death.

—Romans 8:1–2 HCSB

For you did not receive a spirit of slavery to fall back into fear, but you received the Spirit of adoption, by whom we cry out, "*Abba*, Father!"

—Romans 8:15 HCSB

You were bought at a price; do not become slaves of men.

—1 Corinthians 7:23

Now the Lord is the Spirit; and where the Spirit of the Lord is, there is freedom.

—2 Corinthians 3:17 HCSB

But the man who looks intently into the perfect law that gives freedom, and continues to do this, not forgetting what he has heard, but doing it—he will be blessed in what he does.

—James 1:25

Act as free men, and do not use your freedom as a covering for evil, but use it as bondslaves of God.

—1 Peter 2:16 NASB

About Being Joined with Jesus Christ

For I am convinced that neither death nor life, neither angels nor demons, neither the present nor the future, nor any powers, neither height nor depth, nor anything else in all creation, will be able to separate us from the love of God that is in Christ Jesus our Lord.

—Romans 8:38–39

For as many of you as have been baptized into Christ have put on Christ. There is no Jew or Greek, slave or free, male or female; for you are all one in Christ Jesus. And if you are Christ's, then you are Abraham's seed, heirs according to the promise.

—Galatians 3:27–29 HCSB

$\mathcal{J}$ LOVE YOU, DADDY!

Childlike Worship

> And truly, I reiterate, nothing's small!
> No lily-muffled hum of a summer-bee,
> But finds some coupling with the spinning stars;
> No pebble at your foot, but proves a sphere:
> No chaffinch, but implies the cherubim;
> And (glancing at my own thin, veined wrist)
> In such a little tremor of the blood
> The whole strong clamor of a vehement soul
> Doth utter itself distinct. Earth's crammed with heaven,
> And every common bush afire with God;
> But only he who sees, takes off his shoes—
>
> —ELIZABETH BARRETT BROWNING
> *Aurora Leigh, Seventh Book,* LINES 813–23

EVERY BUSH AFLAME

The thunder of falling water obscured all other sounds as melting snows cascaded down a Colorado mountainside. Balancing on a boulder nearby, I photographed a columbine peeking out from a crag. Then I sat down, inhaled the spray-filled air, and drank in the majesty of springtime. In awestruck silence, I suddenly realized that I was a welcome guest, lounging in a parlor reserved for only the most important company—and my host was the One who created it all.

That boulder was holy ground, holy because of the presence of the Lord Almighty, Maker of the heavens and the earth. No one could have convinced me otherwise, because I heard His voice through thunderous waters, saw His gentleness in delicate flowers, and felt His protection above a perilous precipice. God's presence was real because His fingerprints were all around me. I knew that that scene was no product of chance. I wanted to stand up and shout to the world, "Behold the marvelous works of the Lord! Praise Him! Give Him all the glory due His name!" I wanted to shout His praises, even if I shouted alone. But I didn't. My heart and mind praised Him, but I kept silent. I know that God heard the whisper of my heart, but I wonder if any voice is loud enough to glorify our Creator God as He deserves. If I had shouted, would my voice have been lost in the pounding cascades? Would it have echoed down the canyon for others to hear? Would the angels in heaven have joined my praises in song?

Why don't I shout God's praises from my rooftop? If I did, my neighbors would call the police to come get the crazy lady down. What a shame that honest and spontaneous praise would be viewed as the ravings of a lunatic. Children, however, can get away with such enthusiasm.

LOVING THROUGH PRAISE

When Christine was about five, she climbed to the top of her swing set, waved a banner and shouted repeatedly, "God is always greater!" She believed it, and she wanted everyone to know it so that they could believe too. I watched her from inside the house feeling simultaneously proud and embarrassed, wishing I had her innocent courage.

Her childlike fervor demonstrated how our very beings need to praise the Lord, yet so many of us remain silent. We could praise Him out loud. We could help others see His majesty through our eyes. We could help to open their eyes to God's messages in creation, if we would just allow ourselves the freedom to do it. The Bible tells us that if we keep silent, the rocks will cry out in praise (Luke 19:40). In its beauty and splendor, nature is already crying out the truth about God, as I witnessed that day in the mountains.

> The heavens declare the glory of God;
>   the skies proclaim the work of his hands.
> Day after day they pour forth speech;
>   night after night they display knowledge.
> There is no speech or language
>   where their voice is not heard.
> Their voice goes out into all the earth,
>   their words to the ends of the world.
> —Psalm 19:1–4

Why do we keep silent about what we know to be true? We have the best news that was ever heard—or not heard, to our shame. How can we keep from shouting? For our Abba, our Daddy, is Creator of all. Our God *is* God! As the only creatures made in God's image and saved by His grace, shouldn't our voices be the loudest of all?

LOVING THROUGH OBEDIENCE

In Malawi Africa on a mission trip, Glen was surprised at the attitude of the native people who walked beside him. They were new believers and wanted to be baptized. In the sultry heat, they were taking the Americans to the nearest water hole "just over the hill." They walked for hours and then finally reached the muddy pond. When the first man entered the water to be baptized, his demeanor was calm and serene, but when he came up, he started screaming and cheering. After this happened again and again, the Americans found out that the native people understood that when they were baptized, they would die and be raised to new life in Christ. What they didn't understand was that they would not die physically. They had all made peace with their friends and relatives and had said their final farewells. Glen was overwhelmed to realize that these people, believing that they were giving up their lives, were anxious to be baptized. They believed God required it of them, and they were willing to obey.

The apostle Paul urged us to become living sacrifices to God (Rom. 12:1). While still living, we are to become totally His.

LOVING THROUGH COMMUNICATION

Stooping in the tall grass, Steve studied a robber fly and wrote notes about its actions and prey. I watched him, wondering at his patience and admiring his good looks. He glanced up at me. "What are you thinking right now?"

He didn't need to ask. In the months we had been dating, we had both soaked in every word the other said. Like many other couples, we had reached the point where we felt we could read each other's thoughts.

"I was just thinking of how much I love you."

"I love you too."

It didn't matter what we were doing. Spending time together was our deepest desire and our greatest fulfillment during the months before our wedding. Loving each other overshadowed everything else.

Just as in courtship and marriage, our relationship with Jesus thrives when we spend time with Him. As part of the church, His beloved bride, we grow closer to Him in His presence, as we express our deepest thoughts candidly in prayer and soak up every word He says.

When my daughter was young, I was writing a children's musical about prayer and wanted to hear a child's perspective. As we sat on her bed discussing the topic, Christine stated what appeared to be her final word on prayer. "Conversation never stops with God. You don't say 'Amen' until you go to sleep."

Whether she realized it or not, Christine had grasped a truth that often eludes adults. Prayer is not just a few minutes or hours of talking to God. It's not even time set aside to pray, read the Bible, and listen for the Holy Spirit's promptings. Paul tells us to "Pray without ceasing" (1 Thess. 5:17 NASB). If we never cease to pray, then all of life is a prayer, a continuous communing with God.

LOVING IN AWE

When my nephew Teddy was seven, his mother asked him what he would do if Jesus were standing right in front of him. Without a word, Teddy fell facedown on the floor with his arms outstretched. Young children understand the awesomeness of God.

How would I respond in God's presence? I used to imagine Jesus greeting me at the Pearly Gates with a nice warm hug. But the more I know about God, the more I think that when I face my Creator, I will feel compelled to fall down in worship with a mixture of terror, ecstasy, gratitude, and love.

LOVING IN INNOCENCE

The sermon was over and we had begun our second round of worship singing. I noticed that the lady who sat beside me got up and left. A few minutes later, she returned with her toddler son. I assumed she wanted to beat the after-church nursery rush. She held the child, less than two years old, in her arms. We finished the second-to-last song, and the pastor came to the platform for the benediction. Suddenly, the silence was broken by a pure, gentle voice singing, "I will praise You, Lord . . ." It was the little boy beside me continuing the last song. His arms were bent at the elbow as he held up his chubby little hands. My spirit soared as I realized that God had given me the special gift of being one of only a few who had heard the Scripture once again being fulfilled, "Out of the mouth of infants and nursing babies You have prepared praise for Yourself" (Matt. 21:16 NASB). I found out later that his parents always pick him up for the praise singing, because he enjoys it so much.

Yes, it is the little children who understand what it means to love God.

Loving in Infinite Intimacy

Think of your closest relationships. God wants intimacy with us that is closer than any human relationship. Jesus described us in John 15 as branches on the Vine of Himself. Just as the branches on a grapevine would die without the sap flowing from the main vine, we would die spiritually without our intimate connection with our Creator. Hold on firmly to Him. Delight in Him. Relish your life in His Presence.

Celebrating Love!

Our daughter had just turned four and her little friends had come over to celebrate. After the party, they congregated outside in the crisp evening air of early autumn, spinning to see how wide the long, flared skirts of their party dresses could fly. The wind and the golden rays of the setting sun summoned, and when the little girls could no longer contain their exuberance, they ran barefoot around and around our mountain ash tree, trailing their loosened hair ribbons behind them. Watching them, the adults witnessed joyous abandon personified.

A life filled with Jesus is a life of joyous abandon when we give ourselves permission to experience it like a child. Oh, to be able to release our inhibitions to the wind and praise Him with every breath, every inclination of soul, every tremor of spirit! Let's do all we can to worship Him with childlike faith, with the spirit of freedom, and with complete and unreserved love. It will be like experiencing a taste of heaven on earth, like running barefoot across soft grass and flying into Infinite Love's embrace—like running barefoot on holy ground.

> How sweet is the love of my Saviour!
> 'Tis boundless and deep as the sea;
> And best of it all, it is daily
> Growing sweeter and sweeter to me.
>
> I know He is ever beside me!
> Eternity only will prove

The height and the depth of His mercy,
And the breadth of His infinite love.

Wherever He leads I will follow,
Thru sorrow, or shadow, or sun;
And though I be tried in the furnace,
I can say, "Lord, Thy will be it done."

Someday face to face I shall see Him,
And oh, what a joy it will be
To know that His love, now so precious,
Will forever grow sweeter to me!

Sweeter and sweeter to me
Dearer and dearer each day;
Oh, wonderful love of my Saviour
Growing dearer each step of my way!
—CHARLES H. GABRIEL
"GROWING DEARER EACH DAY"

CHILD'S PLAY

1. Run barefoot on soft grass or sand. Imagine yourself running to Jesus, and thank Him for loving you so completely.
2. If you play an instrument, compose a melody of praise from your heart to the Lord. Don't be afraid of what it sounds like to others. Make it as beautiful as you can, and let your love rise up on the wings of the music. Your sincere melody of praise will be a symphony to your heavenly Daddy's ears.
3. Be still and *know* that He is God (see Ps. 46:10).
4. Take a hymnal and find a hymn that expresses the love you are feeling for God. Sing the first verse in your normal voice. Sing the second verse in a quiet, worshipful voice. Then let your voice build to a glorious crescendo on the third and fourth verses, as you praise God from the depths of your soul.

5. Give yourself permission to fall in love with God again. Think about Him, talk with Him, and learn about Him during every spare moment. Then enjoy your newfound romance with your Creator.

6. Even if it isn't Valentine's Day, make a valentine for God. On it, list the things you appreciate about Him most. Wave it toward heaven as if you were launching your words from the paper into the firmament. Then turn your list into a litany. For instance say:

> For your faithfulness, I love You, Lord.
> For your creativity, I love You, Lord.
> For loving me first, I love You, Lord.

7. As part of the body of Christ, you are engaged to the most incredible Person in the universe. Rejoice, celebrate, have a party! Someday soon we will celebrate together at the wedding supper of the Lamb (Rev. 19:9). Anticipate it. Relish it. Tell everyone you know that one day soon, Jesus will take you home to live with Him forever.

DADDY SAYS SO

About Worship

> Ascribe to the LORD the glory due his name;
> worship the LORD in the splendor of his holiness.
>
> —Psalm 29:2

> By day the LORD directs his love,
> at night his song is with me—
> a prayer to the God of my life.
>
> —Psalm 42:8

But I am like an olive tree
     flourishing in the house of God;
I trust in God's unfailing love
     for ever and ever.

—Psalm 52:8

Come, let us bow down in worship,
     let us kneel before the LORD our Maker;
for he is our God
     and we are the people of his pasture,
     the flock under his care.

—Psalm 95:6–7

Shout for joy to the LORD, all the earth.
     Worship the LORD with gladness;
     come before him with joyful songs.

—Psalm 100:1–2

I delight greatly in the LORD;
     my soul rejoices in my God.
For he has clothed me with garments of salvation
     and arrayed me in a robe of righteousness,
as a bridegroom adorns his head like a priest,
     and as a bride adorns herself with her jewels.

—Isaiah 61:10

Love the Lord your God with all your heart and with all your soul
and with all your mind and with all your strength.

—Mark 12:30

I pray that you, being rooted and established in love, may have power, together with all the saints, to grasp how wide and long and high
and deep is the love of Christ, and to know this love that surpasses
knowledge—that you may be filled to the measure of all the fullness
of God.

Now to him who is able to do immeasurably more than all we ask or imagine, according to his power that is at work within us, to him be glory in the church and in Christ Jesus throughout all generations, for ever and ever! Amen.

—Ephesians 3:17–21

Though you have not seen him, you love him; and even though you do not see him now, you believe in him and are filled with an inexpressible and glorious joy, for you are receiving the goal of your faith, the salvation of your souls.

—1 Peter 1:8–9

$\mathcal{N}$OTES

CHAPTER 1: LOOK, DADDY!

1. Cheryn Brewer, letter to Jeanne Gowen Dennis, August 10, 2005.

CHAPTER 3: MY DADDY TAKES CARE OF ME

1. Beth Lagerborg, MOPS newsletter, May 24, 2002.
2. Karen Whiting, e-mail message to Jeanne Gowen Dennis, March 25, 2005.

CHAPTER 4: MY DADDY CAN DO ANYTHING

1. Lois B. Eades, "My Psalm." Used by permission.
2. From the Gaither song, "Something Beautiful," words by Gloria Gaither, music by William J. Gaither (William J. Gaither, Inc., 1971).
3. "He took him outside and said, 'Look up at the heavens and count the stars—if indeed you can count them.' Then he said to him, 'So shall your offspring be.'" (Gen. 15:5)

CHAPTER 5: THAT'S MY DADDY!

1. Janet Holm McHenry, e-mail message to Jeanne Gowen Dennis, March 25, 2005.

CHAPTER 6: I'M SORRY, DADDY

1. C. S. Lewis, *"The Weight of Glory" and Other Addresses* (New York: Touchstone, 1975), 26.

CHAPTER 9: DADDY, HOLD ME!

1. Lee McDowell, interview with Jeanne Gowen Dennis, January 15, 2004.
2. McDowell, interview.
3. Sandra Aldrich, e-mail message to Jeanne Gowen Dennis, July 2005.

CHAPTER 12: DADDY, YOU'RE WONDERFUL!

1. "For the creation was subjected to frustration, not by its own choice, but by the will of the one who subjected it, in hope that the creation itself will be liberated from its bondage to decay and brought into the glorious freedom of the children of God. We know that the whole creation has been groaning as in the pains of childbirth right up to the present time." (Rom. 8:20–22)

CHAPTER 14: LOOK OUT, DADDY, HERE I COME!

1. Louise Tucker Jones, "Dancing Barefoot." Used by permission.